# THE MEDICO-CHIRURGICAL
## SOCIETY OF GLASGOW,
### 1814-1907.

———

#### WALKER DOWNIE.

# THE
# MEDICO-CHIRURGICAL SOCIETY
# OF GLASGOW,
## 1814-1907.

### Presidential Address

*DELIVERED AT THE OPENING MEETING OF THE SESSION
ON 6th OCTOBER, 1907.*

BY

## WALKER DOWNIE, M.B., F.F.P.S.G.,

PRESIDENT OF THE SOCIETY; FELLOW OF THE ROYAL SOCIETY OF MEDICINE, LONDON;
MEMBER OF THE COUNCIL, AND EXAMINER FOR THE FELLOWSHIP, OF THE
FACULTY OF PHYSICIANS AND SURGEONS, GLASGOW; LECTURER ON
DISEASES OF THE THROAT AND NOSE, UNIVERSITY OF GLASGOW
AND WESTERN INFIRMARY; HON. AURIST, ROYAL
HOSPITAL FOR SICK CHILDREN.

GLASGOW:
PRINTED BY ALEX. MACDOUGALL, 68 MITCHELL STREET.
1908.

# CONTENTS.

——o——

# THE MEDICO-CHIRURGICAL SOCIETY OF GLASGOW, 1814-1907.

————◆————

### INTRODUCTORY.

Gentlemen,—The meeting of to-night is not only the first meeting of a new session, but it also marks the beginning of a new chapter in the life-history of this Society.

Many of you are cognisant of the steps taken by this Society, and the Pathological and Clinical Society of Glasgow towards the end of last session, with the object of arranging for the amalgamation of the two Societies.

The proposal emanated from the Pathological and Clinical Society, and it was considered favourably by the Council of the Medico-Chirurgical Society. After several meetings of the committees appointed by the Councils of the respective Societies, the conditions of union were agreed upon by them, the suggested arrangements were in turn submitted to a meeting of the Medico-Chirurgical Society held on 5th April, 1907, at which, on the recommendation of the Council, they were accepted, and the amalgamation was, as a result, successfully concluded. " That amalgamation shall take effect from the beginning of next winter session," is one of the clauses in the agreement, and so the amalgamation is consummated to-night.

As this is not the first time on which our Society has absorbed another society having similar objects, I thought, when casting about for a topic on which I

A

might address you to-night, that a glance at the history
of this Society might not be out of place.  The occasion
seemed opportune for the choice of this as a subject, and
it may be that some facts regarding the life and work of
this Society in days gone by will interest you as members
of it.

There have been in the past, as there now is, several
societies in Glasgow instituted for the discussion of
medical topics ; and in order to convey to you a true record
of this Society, it will be necessary for me to refer shortly,
and by the way to some of the others.

### THE GLASGOW UNIVERSITY MEDICO-CHIRURGICAL SOCIETY, 1802.

In 1802 the Glasgow University Medico-Chirurgical
Society was founded.   It was, and still is, a Society of
undergraduates, at least its ordinary membership is
practically confined to students of medicine, and many
of us in former times were, I am sure, members of it.
During those one hundred and five years, with an ever-
changing ordinary membership, it has continued its career
of usefulness unbroken, and its vigour is still equal to the
proverbial vitality of the student of medicine.

I make mention of this Society, because it appears to
be the first society of the kind in Glasgow of which, at
least, any record can be found : and it goes to show that
the undergraduate felt the necessity, and saw the advantages, of discussing subjects connected with his studies
several years before the graduate in medicine or the
licentiate in surgery thought of meeting formally together
for mutual instruction.

### THE GLASGOW MEDICAL SOCIETY, 1814.

On 27th October, 1814, there met " by mutual agreement " the following six gentlemen, viz., Dr. Watt,
Dr. Graham, Dr. Robertson, Mr. Pattison, Mr. John

Young, and Mr. M'Leod, presumably three physicians and three surgeons, and Dr. Watt was unanimously voted to the chair.

They had met for the purpose of forming a society, and after the subject had been discussed, they agreed upon the following resolutions :—

"That the Society be nominated 'The Glasgow Medical and Surgical Society.'

"That the Society be exclusively for the prosecution of 'Medical Science.'

"That a paper or essay be read at each meeting, the subject of said paper or essay alone to be discussed during that meeting, but that four quarterly meetings be allotted for the discussion of the then prevalent diseases and those which have occurred during the preceding three months.

"That an annual president, two vice-presidents, a treasurer, and a secretary be elected by vote.

"A committee of three was then resolved on, and Dr. Watt, Dr. Graham, and Dr. Robertson were chosen, and they were ordered to draw up a series of laws to be presented for the consideration and amendment of the Society at next meeting.

"It was further resolved on, that entry money, a fine for want of paper or essay, and a fine for absence or being late, be levied, and that a meeting of the Society take place on the 4th November."

At the second meeting it was moved by Dr. Graham and seconded by Dr. Monteath "that as the name Glasgow Medical and Surgical Society is objectionable to some of its members, the resolution imposing that appellation shall further be considered at next meeting," and in the minutes of next meeting the bare statement occurs, "It is resolved that the name of the Society be altered to that of the Glasgow Medical Society." Astonishment might be expressed at the choice of "Medical" as against "Medical and Surgical" for the title of the young Society.   It seems as unreasonable as it is misleading, for the Society contained surgeons as well as physicians, and the papers read and discussed by its members dealt with surgical subjects equally with those which might be considered to be of a purely medical character.  But some members apparently had a strong objection to couple surgery with medicine, and the explanation may be found in the fact that at this time there was considerable friction between the University and the Faculty of Physicians and Surgeons, regarding the rights of University graduates in medicine to practise surgery.  At this time the number of graduates in medicine was increasing rapidly, chiefly on account of the very easy conditions under which they were then able to obtain that degree.  By reason of their number they were of necessity compelled to leave the traditional lines of the pure physician, and to take to general practice, including the practice of surgery.  The Faculty had noted this great influx of practitioners, for there were graduates of Edinburgh, of Aberdeen, and of St. Andrews, as well as of the University of Glasgow, and who, while resident within its borders, were yet not under its jurisdiction or supervision; and the Faculty was at this date on the eve of testing the legality of the position of those practitioners.  In the following year, in fact, the Faculty did raise the question before the Court of Session, the crux of the matter being, " Does a degree in medicine confer the right to practise surgery?"  It was the beginning of a lawsuit which lasted for fourteen years, and engendered a feeling of hostility between the opposing bodies which long remained more or less active.

An interesting account of the trial, with its bearings on the subsequent history of the Faculty, is given by Dr. Alexander Duncan in his valuable " Memorials of the Faculty of Physicians and Surgeons."  The decision did not cover the whole ground of the pleadings, but it was decided so far in favour of the pursuers that " the degrees in question did not so qualify within the bounds of the Faculty."

The title of "The Glasgow Medical Society" was for the time being adopted. Five years later, however, there appears in the minutes of a meeting, held on 15th October, 1819, a proposal "that, as there exists in Glasgow another and an older society of the same name with this Society, and as this one originally was named the 'Glasgow Medical and Surgical,' that it shall in future be called 'The Glasgow Medical and Surgical Society.'" It was an attempt apparently on the part of the surgeons to assert the importance of their branch of the healing art. The motion was, without any reason being assigned, subsequently withdrawn, and Dr. Duncan gives the opinion that "there was probably no valid ground for the statement in the motion, as it is hardly conceivable that the title of an older existing society should have been assumed, or that, when the matter was challenged, the usurpation of the title should have been persisted in." "The probability is," he says "that the association to which allusion is made was the 'Glasgow Medical Club.'"

## PLACE OF MEETING.

No record can be found to indicate the place at which the first four meetings of the Society were held; but at the third meeting it was moved "that application be made, at the first meeting of Faculty, for the use of their hall." As a result of this application the Faculty, at its meeting in December, 1814, unanimously granted to the Glasgow Medical Society the use of its hall.

The Faculty of Physicians and Surgeons has ever been ready to lend its rooms for meetings of professional and scientific societies, or for the discussion of questions bearing on medicine and surgery. And so the privilege granted was taken as a matter of course, and no vote of thanks is recorded. More than this, the members of the Medical Society, while enjoying the hospitality of the Faculty to the extent of sitting rent-free, did in 1826,

what I fear we, similarly accommodated, sometimes do,
gave vent to a grumble. They made complaint of the
coldness and uncomfortable condition of the hall, and a
committee was appointed to enquire into the matter, and
see whether it would be better to attempt some alterations or to find some other room in town better adapted
to the purpose. No mention is made of the subject in
any subsequent minute ; and, looking to the small balance
in the treasurer's hands at this time, I think they were
wise to remain the uncomplaining guests of the Faculty.

## ADMISSION OF STRANGERS.

When the question of a title for the Society had been
settled, a fresh subject for difference of opinion was
found in the subject of admission of strangers.

At an early meeting, a " motion was submitted, enact-
ing a law regarding the admission of strangers, viz., that
the members of the Society shall have it in their power
to introduce strangers, who reside at least five miles
from Glasgow." But, two meetings later, whether on
account of the excessive number of strangers interested
in the discussions, and introduced by the members, or not,
is not disclosed, the motion, when brought up, was altered
as follows :—" The essayist shall alone have the power
of introducing not more than two strangers, and which
strangers must reside at least five miles from Glasgow."
This motion, however, when put to the vote at the meeting at which it was discussed two months later, was
rejected, and the subject of admission of strangers was
allowed to drop.

Some years later (1828) the question was revived by a
motion laid on the table, signed by six members—the proposal being that any member should have the privilege
of introducing a non-resident medical friend to the ordinary meetings of the Society—but when this motion came
up for discussion it was negatived.

## FINES AND PENALTIES.

A reader perusing the early records of the Society might be pardoned if he came to the conclusion that the chief objects of this, the first, society of medical men in Glasgow, were, the compulsory reading of a paper by each member in rotation, and the imposition of fines for negligence and non-attendance.

The first penalty to be noted is under the heading of office-bearers. "A member must accept office, or incur the penalty of one guinea." The ordinary members are next warned that "the roll shall be called, and such as are absent shall incur the fine of two shillings, unless sick or three miles distant from town; one-half to be remitted on the member entering the room within half an hour after the business has commenced."

A year later this rule was altered to the effect that "The roll shall be immediately called, and again after the essay is read; or at quarterly meetings at 9 o'clock, the fine for absence, at each time, being one shilling."

But the terrors of the law were reserved for the essayist. The first rule under this title is that "Essays shall be read by members in rotation," and the description of the communication so required of him is, "A paper or essay may either be in the form of a dissertation, or the detail of a case with annotations, written by the person whose turn it is to present one, by a substitute, or a friend not a member of the Society. The subject must be submitted to the Society for approval two months before being read, under a penalty of half a guinea, and it cannot be changed without permission, and the payment of a fine of five shillings," except in certain cases which are specified. "Any member who is allowed to take for his substitute a resident member, shall pay for the indulgence the fine of five shillings." And then we come to the climax. "The essay so prepared must be handed to the secretary at the meeting previous to

that at which it should be read, and if it is not given in
on the night appointed, the essayist shall incur the
penalty of half a guinea; if not read on the night it is due
he shall pay one guinea additional; if he does not read it
at the second meeting, two guineas more; if not at the
third, he shall, besides, cease to be a member of the
Society."

I am sure that both our general secretary and our
treasurer would almost wish for the power to revive at
least some of these penal clauses.

Another ground on which a fine might be levied was
discovered in the action of Mr. Clark, who had added
some pages to his essay shortly before reading it. As he
thus had not laid "an entire essay" on the table, he consequently incurred the fine of half a guinea, and the
meeting agreed by a small majority that the fine should
be imposed. But at this stage Mr. Brown rose and
moved that, "as Mr. Clark might not at the time have
been aware of having infringed the laws, the said fine
be remitted," and this was carried by a large majority.

While some members demurred to the payment of the
fines incurred, others seemed to consider their payment
a pleasant duty. Thus we read that Dr Young, "agree-
able to the promise made by the treasurer, sent his essay
to the hall as early as it was in his power, namely, on
the ninth day after last meeting; and in conformity to
the strict letter of the law, paid his fine of ten shillings
and sixpence."

Again, Mr. Cowan, "who was confined by indisposi-
tion, informed the Society that he was not perpared to
lay his essay on the table, but that it would be transmitted as soon as possible, and the fine paid."

At the meeting held on 1st December, 1818, Dr.
William Couper did not attend, nor did he announce the
subject of his essay, and the secretary was directed to
inform him that "he had consequently incurred the fine
of half a guinea according to the laws." But Dr. Couper

having at the next meeting explained the causes of his absence, the Society agreed to remit the fine, and at the same time they received the title of his essay. It was, " What proofs have been adduced in support of the theory of compression in the consolidation of mineral strata." What exactly followed the reading of that paper is not recorded, but Mr. M'Leod proposed that the essay should be left with Mr. Jones (who was the officer of the Faculty, and acted in the same capacity to this Society), so that the members might have an opportunity of reading it in the hall, which motion was unanimously carried.

At the following meeting Dr. Couper intimated that " he did not find it convenient to continue a member of this Society." The name of Dr. William Couper occurs three times in the list of members, and as there are no distinguishing features regarding either the name or the title, it must be assumed that the same gentleman is indicated. He was re-elected a short time after the above incident, but in 1821 a letter was received from him requesting that " his name be erased from the list of members." Again he was elected, and in 1825 he again resigned ; and shortly thereafter he was elected an honorary member, thus escaping the necessity for paying further election expenses.

The relationship between this gentleman and the honorary membership of the Society makes one think of the association supposed to exist between a troublesome member of Parliament and the House of Lords.

To prepare an essay under compulsion, and to read the same to members of a Society who were present in order that they might thereby escape the payment of a fine imposed for non-attendance, does not sound an inviting occupation, and one would imagine could not be conducive to good work or hearty discussion. But in a small society it was necessary that each member should take an active part, and the larger the audience the greater would be the stimulus to the essayist to give of his best, and the result, as seen in the thirty-one large volumes of Transactions in manuscript now in the safe keeping of the Faculty, is a worthy record of the industry and professional attainments of our predecessors.

I think that the system of fines, while it proved irksome on some occasions, was, on the whole, beneficial to the Society in its early days—later it was harmful. The senior members, as they became more engrossed in the practice of their profession or in research work, and others who were teachers and delivered their lectures in the evening, found it impossible to attend the meetings with regularity. They, therefore, in many cases found it more convenient, and possibly more economical, to resign their membership, than to pay the penalty imposed for absence.

## MEETINGS AND LEAVE OF ABSENCE.

For the first eighteen months after the formation of the Society, two statutory meetings were held each month throughout the whole year. As attendance at each meeting was imperative under penalty of a fine, we can sympathise with those members who were busily engaged in family practice or who desired when the days were long to take more than a week-end in the country. Any member who desired to be released from attendance required to make application to this effect, stating the reason for the application. Among the earlier applications we have the following :—" In consequence of Dr. Perry's application for leave of absence from the Society during the season, Dr. Monteath moved that such leave be granted to him, seconded by Mr. Watson." I did not at first quite grasp the meaning of the word " season " here used, as the application was made under date 5th December; but as leave could not be granted to him until the subject had been brought before the meeting to

be held on 19th December, the application was made, I
have no doubt, in view of the near approach of the Christ-
mas festivities. It is interesting to learn from the
minutes of the latter meeting that as a result of his
timeous application, "leave of absence during the
season" was granted to Dr. Perry. I could find no note
of any member having made application, during the year
of Waterloo, for leave of absence to go to the seat of war.

Frequent, and in some instances periodical, applications for leave of absence were made, and while the
reason assigned was occasionally questioned, the leave
was, without exception, so far as I could find, formally
granted.

Dr. William Mackenzie, who was elected an ordinary
member in January, 1820, and who at a later period was
appointed oculist to Queen Victoria, presented a letter at
the first meeting of the next session—that is, in October,
1820—requesting leave of absence from the Society during
the session, which was granted without remark. But when
a letter was received from Dr. Robertson, stating that
" he could not attend the meetings of the Society till the
conclusion of the course of clinical lectures in which he
was engaged," he was reminded " that he should have
presented a paper at this meeting," and the Society
directed the secretary to inform him that " though they
were willing to give him leave of absence for the time
specified, they still consider him bound to produce and
read his paper according to the regulations." The reply
was an intimation of Dr. Robertson's resignation. In
the following year he was re-elected ; and so it appears to
have been with others, resignation, when attendance was
inconvenient, followed by re-election after a time.

This method of shirking one of the duties of membership seemed to be on the increase until 1840, when
it was enacted " that any gentleman resigning his membership of the Society, during the session when his name
stands in the list of essayists, shall be considered as

having been dismissed, unless a reason, satisfactory to the Society, shall be assigned for doing so."

Re-admission also had become a very simple process, for in January, 1839, the following alteration in the law relating to this subject was passed by ballot, viz., " All former members of the Society may be re-elected into the Society by the vote of the majority, without the payment of a new entrance fee. The previous period of membership shall be reckoned part of the period which exempts from payment of fines and reading of essays." But in the application of this rule, even in its modified form, laxity crept in, and the necessity for closer adherence to the laws was thought necessary. In 1843 Dr. Watson was re-admitted as a member of the Society, but " it was agreed that his election, and that of Dr. Brown, on the night of proposal, should not be made a precedent for the re-election of any other old member, but that the law requiring the names of members to lie on the table should be enforced in all cases."

Dr. Mackenzie was a member for over two years before he submitted his first essay to the Society, which was entitled, " Remarks contributive to the natural history of puro-mucous inflammation of the conjunctiva." Dr. Mackenzie was most regular in making application for " the leave of absence usually granted to those occupied in the delivery of lectures." The Society apparently questioned the reason assigned, for the secretary was requested " to inform Mr. Mackenzie that his non-attendance would be excused, provided he was actually engaged in the delivery of his lectures during the hour of the Society's meetings."

## SUMMER RECESS.

Others besides those whose names I have mentioned began to feel the strain of these regularly recurring fortnightly meetings throughout the whole year; and on 16th

April, 1816, Dr. Watt, who had been the first President, moved that "the meetings of the Society shall be adjourned from the third Tuesday of May until the first Tuesday of October annually," and the proposal was at a subsequent meeting carried by a majority.

## OPTIONAL SUMMER MEETINGS.

But some members, it would appear, began to feel lonely when summer days were long and the visiting lists were short, and they pined to meet their fellows in friendly conversation. As a consequence, three years later, it was agreed that the Society should hold meetings on the first Tuesday of June, July, August, and September, these meetings to be spent in professional conversations, and it is added, "it being understood that attendance at these meetings should not be compulsory."

And later (in 1827) it was agreed to appoint a committee of five members, who should meet once a month during the summer recess and prepare a report on the state of the weather, the prevailing diseases and their relative mortality during each month ; the information so acquired to be condensed in a report to be read at the first meeting in October, and if thought expedient by the Society to be printed and distributed amongst the members.

## SUBJECTS OF DISCUSSION.

The range of subjects discussed by our predecessors in those early days was even wider than we now permit ourselves, and in purely medical subjects they ranged from the essay by Mr. M'Leod, read at a very early meeting, "On Dyspepsia as occurring in himself," to "Malignant cholera," which was rife in the city in 1832. Cases of "Irregular hysteria" were dealt with, as were "Ulcers as they occur on board of the King's ships." There was a paper on "Blue devils," another on the

" Case of a fasting woman." Dr. Duncan tells us that
the author of the latter essay, Mr. George Macleod, was
a Highlander with a lofty appreciation of the Celtic race.
In discussing the bona fides of the patient, who, he
admitted, had not been properly watched so as to place
the element of deception beyond doubt, he inclined to
the opinion that the abstinence from food was real ; and
in favour of this view he naively urged, " She was a very
religious woman, to which may be added the circumstance
of her being a Highland woman, for I believe that those
of Celtic extraction are less apt to impose on the public
than others." Other subjects were cases of " Dysphagia
from ulcerated glottis," case of " Ulcerated epiglottis,"
" Cases of Bronchotomy," " Papers on Iritis," " On the
non-mercurial treatment of syphilis," " On Spina
Bifida," and " On the dilation of the pupil by narcotics."
Then we find Dr. A. D. Anderson on two separate occasions describing " Unsuccessful cases in surgery," which
example is not so often followed nowadays as it might
be. Remarks on " Medical education," on " Medical
ethics," on " The removal of vesical calculi without
incision," " On some of the most important indigenous
medical plants and their preparations," "On the medical
charity of Glasgow," and " The mortality of children
under one year," which apparently gave rise to concern
then as it does in the present time.

## TRANSFUSION.

Then we find Dr. Lyon urging the necessity for transfusion in post-partum uterine hæmorrhage, and stating
his belief that many lives otherwise sacrificed might be
saved ; and he showed a simple apparatus for purposes
of transfusion, which he had devised, consisting of a
common dissecting blow-pipe and a common bladder.

## ETHER, 1847.

In February, 1847, an interesting professional conversation took place regarding the merits of the new remedy of inhalation of ether for the mitigation of painful operations.

Dr. Perry, in opening the discussion, said he had seen ether used, and he noticed that it produced intoxication of a peculiar kind, and during which it had the effect of bringing out the characters of the individuals. He had seen it produce nausea and vomiting sufficient to prevent its continued inhalation. It was uncertain, and varied in different individuals, both in the time necessary to produce the effects, and the duration and intensity of those effects, but he considered it a most important remedy. He cautioned any from using it by candle light, as the vapour was very combustible. In one case he was applying it to a lady, when a servant approached with a candle to a distance of 4 or 6 feet, with the result that the vapour took fire and they were all enveloped in a blaze, which fortunately was but instantaneous. Dr. Hall considered that the effects of ether were similar to those of alcohol, differing only in degree ; Dr. Bell was afraid that the inhalation of a large quantity of ether would cause worse effects than the pain of an operation ; whereas Mr. Miller, from his experience of it in hospital, thought that the cases of success were so numerous there could now be no doubt regarding the value of the remedy.

## CHLOROFORM, 1848.

In January, 1848, a discussion on Chloroform took place. It was introduced by Dr. Adams, the secretary, who had made many trials of the new anæsthetic agent. The results were such as to make him fear that its use would not be so extensive nor its benefits so certain as was commonly alleged, and under any circumstance its use required caution and discrimination in the choice of cases. Dr. Miller thought that Dr. Adams had been unfortunate in his cases, and Dr. Lyon thought that he took too unfavourable a view of the new remedy.   Dr. Lyon then described several cases, amputation of the thigh, etc., in which he had had it administered, and so favourably had he been impressed, that if he had to undergo a severe operation himself he would have the chloroform used.   Dr. Bell, on the other hand, said that, as far as he had heard of the new remedy, he thought that few of the members would feel disposed to use it in their own families, for many effects described were worse than an operation.

Two years later Mr. Lyon reports details of a case which had proved fatal in his hands under the use of chloroform, and where the immediate application of every remedy which could be thought of at the time, including artificial respiration, bleeding from the jugular, tracheotomy and galvanism, had failed to produce the slightest manifestation of life.   Many spoke adversely of its use, particularly in private, where that assistance, obtainable in hospital, could not be had; and Dr. Adams said that, "from communications he had had from friends in Edinburgh, he learned that the statements issued regarding the uniform and perfect success and safety of its use in that place were not unimpeachable."

The deliverance of Dr. Easton, then Professor of Materia Medica in Anderson's College, is interesting on account of the position he occupied both then and later. It is as follows:—"Here we have a case in which chloroform is employed by an individual experienced in its use, and with all the ready appliances of a public hospital at hand, and yet death occurs so completely and so instantaneously that the case is remediless."  "The deduction to be drawn from such a case is, that we are not warranted in proceeding further with the use of this remedy."

But with this position Mr. Lyon could not agree.  "He was not inclined to say that the use of chloroform should be abandoned. He had seen it used fully one hundred times, and, with the exception of certain fatal cases, including his own, he had not observed what could be called bad effects from its use. On the other hand, it was difficult to over-estimate the amount of positive pain which had been mitigated or avoided by its employment. We had not yet sufficient experience of the remedy to abandon it. It might be that we would arrive at a better knowledge of its properties, and have it more completely in command. He was rather inclined to recommend that when used it should be employed exclusively under the superintendence of an experienced assistant, whose sole duty should be that of administering the drug."

We cannot but admire the firm and statesmanlike attitude of Mr. Lyon. It required a strong man and a brave man to speak as he did under the conditions then existing. His statement further shows that he recognised thus early the absolute necessity for the chloroformist devoting his undivided attention to the administration of the anæsthetic.

Chloroform was again discussed in March, 1852, at the instigation of the president, who requested an expression of the opinion of members on the question of whether the employment of the drug was on the increase or the decline.

One member said he had not used, and did not intend to use it. Few had had experience of it in obstetrics. But Mr. Lyon recounted a case wherein he was required to turn the child, and here he had used chloroform with decided benefit. "At the same time," he said, "it was right to bear in mind that our Professor of Midwifery (Dr. Pagan) thought that such an agent should not be used in cases of this nature, where the patient, by being rendered insensible, was unable to guide us as to her sensations." Dr. Robertson had no experience of chloroform in midwifery, and this from his conviction that it was unnecessary in natural labour and injurious in instrumental labour; but in surgical cases he thought that its use had

B

conferred a great boon upon humanity. And Mr. Lyon
again said that so much knowledge of its use, and caution
in its administration, were required, that he would not
operate on a patient unless the chloroform was administered by a medical man, and one experienced in its use at
the same time.

## TYPHUS FEVER, 1835.

Dr. Robert Perry, who has already been referred to,
was an original member of the Medical Society, and one
who took a very active part in its proceedings throughout
his whole professional life. He was a physician to the
Royal Infirmary and to the Fever Hospital in Clyde
Street. As a result of original investigations in the latter
institution, he submitted to this Society " a series of pro-
positions which establish a strong case," as Dr. Duncan
expresses it, " in favour of his priority in the recognition
of the non-identity of typhus and typhoid fever," and in
1835 a commission was appointed by this Society to visit
the wards of the Fever Hospital, along with Dr. Perry,
who readily undertook to point out the facts upon which
his opinions had been formed.

Some years later (1847), during a discussion on typhus
fever, one of the points at issue had reference to the con-
tagiousness of typhus, and Dr. Perry described an experiment he had made, which appeared to settle the question.
" He had succeeded," he said, " about six years ago in
inoculating typhus, and had since repeated the experiment
with success. He had rubbed cotton upon the skin of a
typhus patient, at the time desquamation was going on,
and then introduced the cotton into the nostrils of another
person." " The experiment," he remarks, " was quite
safe when tried on children." This may have been justi-
fiable in those days in the attempt to modify typhus, which
was then so rife, by inducing an attack in youth; but
to-day experiments conducted on those lines would bring
the practitioner within the pale of the law.

### CHOLERA, 1849.

The influence of the personal equation in the successful treatment (or is it in the diagnosis?) of disease was as evident then as it is now.   This may here be illustrated by a glimpse at a discussion held in 1849 on the then recent epidemic of cholera.   The discussion became animated in consequence of some statements made by Dr. Hall, and the meeting was adjourned.   At the following meeting, Dr. Hall resumed the discussion, and stated that he had in the interval " consulted his notes and found that his statement of having treated upwards of 200 cases successfully during the late epidemic was incorrect, but that the actual number of cases which had come under his care was 113, and of these only one person had died, a circumstance (i.e., the fatal issue) which was attributed to the patient having neglected to follow up the treatment with regularity, towards the termination of the case."   One would think it was bad enough to die, but much worse that the dead man should be blamed.

Other members who had followed the same line of treatment, viz., that of Dr. Ayre of Hull, stated that their results had been altogether opposed to those furnished by Dr. Hall, and one of the older members, giving his own experience, said " he had found the results of all modes of treatment very unsatisfactory, the mortality having always been about fifty per cent."

### ELECTION DECLARED NULL AND VOID.

The above discussion took place at the 553rd meeting of the Society, and at the 556th meeting Dr. Hall had his revenge.   He questioned the legality of the election of office-bearers which had taken place at the preceding meeting, when only nine members had been present, while ten were necessary to form a quorum.   He had his way, the election was declared null and void, and the proceedings were begun "de novo." The minute of this latter meeting is distinguished by being one of a very few which contains a full list of the members present.

Now the question of a quorum became a burning one, and it was proposed that the rule bearing on this matter should be altered so that "seven members shall form a quorum." But the motion, which gave rise to much discussion, was withdrawn when it was pointed out that the law which regulated the number requisite to form a quorum applied to the transaction of private business only, and did not interfere with the regular transaction of the ordinary public business, such as the reading of essays, professional conversations, etc.

## CHOLERA, 1853.

The meeting which should have been held on the third Tuesday in October, 1853, was postponed in consequence of a meeting of the members of the profession in anticipation of cholera. There is no indication of the conclusions arrived at at this meeting, nor of any preparations made in view of the threatened epidemic; but at a subsequent meeting of the Medical Society it was stated that cholera and choleraic diarrhœa were much more widely diffused and numerically of a much graver aspect than the community, forming its opinion from the limited statistics of the daily papers, supposed.

The feeling of the members of the profession towards this fatal epidemic disease may be gathered from the remarks of Dr. Wilson, made during one of the conversational discussions. He had seen little of the disease during that epidemic, but he thought that in the cases he had seen the cramp was less severe, and he closes his remarks thus, "Inscrutable as yet, and baffling all our attempts, he thought the words of the Psalmist, ' a pestilence walking in darkness,' as a description peculiarly applicable to this malady."

## HOMEOPATHY, 1852.

Early in 1852 there was what might be styled a full dress debate on the subject of homeopathy. It was the outcome of the appointment of a practitioner of homeopathy by the Caledonian Insurance Company to be associated with Drs. Wilson and Watson in their office of medical referees to that Company. In the course of the discussion all the members present took a part, and each expressed himself in strong terms regarding that doctrine. The position of the profession in its relation to the new cult is expressed in two motions :—" That the practice of homeopathy is injurious to the community and opposed to the truths of medical science, and therefore merits the strongest reprobation from the medical profession," and, " That no member of the medical profession can be associated in professional duty with an individual practising homeopathy without injury to medical science and loss of personal character." Descending from the general to the particular, it is recorded that " animadversions were made on the conduct of an individual in Glasgow who practised homeopathy, and also upon the gullibility and the officious meddling of clergymen and the annoyance of which they were frequently the agents between medical men and their patients."

## FUNDS.

The income of the Society was derived from the entrance fee of one guinea, payable by each member on his admission ; and from fines. The latter formed a very substantial proportion of the whole annual income. It is interesting to note that during the sessions 1814-15 and 1815-16 the members were most active in their attendance, in submitting essays and discussing the essays submitted ; that few fines were exacted, and these were imposed chiefly on account of the arrival of the member after the

business of the meeting had commenced, and in some few
cases for absence.

## INTEREST.

As time went on, money was accumulating in the hands
of the treasurer, and in 1820 the treasurer had in hand
£25, 3s. 5½d.  Some member skilled in finance saw the
advantage accruing to the gentleman holding the office of
treasurer, and he proposed that in future the treasurer
should pay interest at the rate of 3½ per cent. on the
balance of cash in his hands.  This was agreed to, and at
the end of the year the treasurer added the sum of 17s. 6d.
as interest.  He was apparently a man of repute, for the
Society did not demand security for the funds.  In 1821
the rate of interest paid was 4 per cent., which yielded £1,
but the money market appeared to become easier, for in
the following year the treasurer was called upon to pay
3 per cent. only, though it rose on several subsequent
occasions to 4 per cent., and in 1835 the rate was reduced
to 2½ per cent.

## FINES.

The income of the Society was, as I have said, derived,
during the first thirty years of its existence, from entrance
fees and from fines.  The proportion which those two
items bear to each other when they are stated separately,
for sometimes they are slumped, may be seen from the
following examples, taken practically at random from the
treasurer's account book :—

| | Balance on hand. | Entrants. | Fines. | Interest. |
|---|---|---|---|---|
| 1828-29, | £37 16  9 | £4  4  0 | £8  0  6 | £1  0  0 |
| 1832-33, | 16 18  7 | 5  5  0 | 9  7  6 | 0  8  6 |
| 1833, | 26  2  5 | 7  7  0 | 11  9  6 | 0 12  0 |

In 1841 fines to the extent of £6, 3s. were paid, and on
looking into the particulars it is seen that this amount
includes the sum of £5 paid by Dr. Hannay, and it is
noted that this is "commutation allowed for arrears."

On further investigation it is found that the said Dr. Hannay was in arrears at that date to the extent of £6, 17s.

The last note of interest having been paid (save one of 14s. on £14, 10s. 5d. in 1865-1866) is in October, 1843, and then at the rate of 3 per cent., and the last fines were paid on 21st January, 1845.

In 1815 a ballot-box was purchased at a cost of £1, 10s., and in the following year a charter chest was procured at a cost of £1, 1s.  No reference to a charter, however, occurs in the minutes until 1865, when it was suggested by Dr. Ritchie in his presidential address.

### SALARY OF OFFICER.

Mr. Jones, the officer, was at first paid £3, 3s. '' for his trouble in connection with the Society.''  Later this was raised to £5, and in 1835 to £6, but when in 1844 the funds in hand became low, on account of many resignations, his honorarium was reduced to £3, 3s.

### SOME ITEMS OF EXPENDITURE.

Amongst items of expenditure peculiar to the times was the regular charge for candles—thus in 1816, 8s. appears under this head.  In 1831 this item disappears, and we find its place taken by a charge of 14s. for '' oil and jar,'' and another of £7, 18s. for lamps.  The expenditure so incurred resulted in a deficit on the year's working of £12, 17s. 7d., but even after this payment there remained a balance in hand of £43, 19s. 7d.  Immediately following on this unusual expenditure, it was proposed to give a sum of £20 for the benefit of the mother, the widow, and family of their recently deceased secretary, Dr. Armour, and this sum was voted unanimously.

### TO EXTEND USEFULNESS OF SOCIETY, 1844.

In 1844 there was a falling off in the membership, few new members were being added, and few remained to pay fines, so the funds were low.  At this stage a special

meeting was called at the request of three members, to
consider if any plan could be adopted to extend the usefulness of the Society, and a committee was appointed for
enquiry and report.  At the meeting at which the report
was submitted, the president read a communication which
he had received from the secretary of the newly formed
Medico-Chirurgical Society of Glasgow, intimating that
they would be happy to admit all the members of the
Medical Society without ballot or any form of election.
The advent of this new society was apparently proving a
strong counter-attraction to the members of the profession
in the city.  No note is made of the nature of the recommendations contained in the report submitted by the committee appointed; but it is stated on 24th July that the
various alterations on the laws which had been approved of
at last meeting were finally adopted, and the only tangible
change which can be gleaned from the records is that
contained in the minutes recording the business of the first
meeting of the following session, which is that " In consequence of the reduced state of the funds, and the small
number of members of the Society at present, it was agreed
that the officer's salary be three guineas, and the treasurer
was instructed to inform Mr. Jones accordingly."

## DRASTIC CHANGES PROPOSED.

Whatever the alterations may have been, they did not
give satisfaction, so that twelve months later fresh notices
of motion were tabled.  They embodied drastic changes
in the constitution.  The first was that, instead of paying
an entry fee of one guinea, it should be optional with
future members to pay five shilings annually; secondly,
that in future the reading of essays shall be voluntary;
and, thirdly, that in future the Society shall meet only on
the first Tuesday of every month.

When these proposals were discussed and voted upon,
the two first were adopted, but the third, curtailing the

number of meetings, was negatived. These alterations
were apparently very popular, for their adoption was
immediately followed by an accession of seventeen new
members.

Members appeared to exercise the option and pay one
guinea on admission on till 1860, at which date the Society
agreed that the entrance fee of one guinea be cancelled,
and, instead, the rule dealing with this subject was made
to read, "When admitted the member must pay five
shillings of entry money, and a further contribution of five
shillings on each succeeding session, and that the admission of perpetual members be discontinued, and that no
commutation of fees be allowed in future."

It is well in this place to make a note of the state of the
funds at the time of amalgamation of this Society with
the Medico-Chirurgical Society, which subject will be
referred to more fully later on. The accounts were presented as follows :—

| | |
|---|---|
| Balance from session 1864-65, . . | £14 10 5 |
| Income for year, . . . . . | 4 19 1 |
| | £19 9 6 |
| Expenses, . . . . . . | 5 14 0 |
| By balance, . . . . . . | £13 15 6 |

The balance of income over the ordinary expenditure
showed that the Society was in quite a healthy financial
condition : and the amount carried forward was greater
than the average credit balance of the previous twenty
years.

## SECRETARIES.

The post of secretary to a Society like this is, to my
mind, a more important one than even that of the presi-
dentship. The names even of the past presidents would
be wholly unknown had not the secretary carefully

recorded them in the minute book; and our knowledge of
the Society and its proceedings hangs entirely on what he
thought fit to enter in the minute book. This Society
during its long career had many secretaries. One died in
office, and the Society valued himself and his services so
highly, that it unanimously voted nearly one-half of its
whole capital to the benefit of his mother, his widow, and
family.

In many instances the secretary has in turn become the
president.

The records transmitted to us are often very meagre;
but with the appointment of Dr. James Adams in 1845 a
change is observed, and his suitability for the post is
evident. The minutes become full and clearly written,
and his records of the proceedings are not only very
interesting, but they strike one as being eminently fair,
judged by the full reports he gives of the remarks of
members, who spoke in direct opposition to his own
opinions formally expressed.

## THE PASSING OF MR. JONES.

A pathetic note is recorded in the first minute of session
1849-1850 to the effect that " Mr. Jones, officer of the
Society, being now incapacitated from the farther exercise
of his duties by age and infirmities, it was remitted to the
president, treasurer, and secretary to make the necessary
arrangements for filling the vacant situation." Whatever appointment was made, the officer is in future
referred to simply as the officer, and only once by name,
and that many years later.

## DISTRIBUTION OF BILLETS.

In 1863, the finance committee of the Faculty intimated
that the billets of this Society could no longer be addressed
and distributed by the Faculty officer; and the only

services to be rendered by him in future were those connected with lighting, heating, and putting the meeting-
rooms in order.  As a consequence it was agreed that the
officer (now Mr. Menzies) should be remunerated in future
with a payment of £2 per annum.

## TO ARRANGE THE "LAWS."

There had been so many alterations made in the laws,
and many more proposed, that much confusion arose in
their interpretation, and in April, 1848, it was resolved
that a committee should be appointed to collect and
arrange the existing laws of the Society, to suggest alterations and amendments on the same, and to report progress
at the first meeting of the next session.  A report was
submitted, but its nature is not divulged.

Early in the session of 1850 a conversation took place on
the subject of the hour of meeting, when the greater
number of the members present expressed themselves in
favour of a change being made from eight to nine o'clock.
But this change, if it was carried out, had no influence in
increasing the attendance of members.  The secretary
seems also to have lost his former enthusiasm, for the
record of the proceedings suddenly becomes most frag-
mentary, and the first volume of minutes closes with the
folowing memorandum, " Meetings were held in April
(1851), but no quorum assembled.  The evenings were
passed in professional conversation."  The minutes of the
next session begin a new volume, and the transactions
are again very fully recorded, and, judged by the number
of speakers who took part in the discussions, some fresh
interest must have been aroused amongst the members in
the work of the Society.

## PROFESSIONAL CONVERSATIONS.

While the formal essays, which were at first contributed
under compulsion, and later under the same conditions as

obtain with ourselves, are from some points instructive even now, I found the reports of the meetings spent in professional conversation much more interesting. The personality of the speaker is often so fully revealed in those informal discussions; his opinions, the style of his practice, and the results he claims are full of interest. While we may have one speaker after another agreeing with the leader of the evening in his opinion of the subject under discussion, and the method of treatment adopted under the conditions described by him, we meet with others, of whom, while it cannot exactly be said that they were "agin' the Government," are opposed on every occasion and on every subject to the author of the essay or conversation. Chief amongst the latter is Dr. John Reid, and as you read the reports of his many remarks —and he always did make remarks when he was present —you can almost see the little red-haired man with thin lips and querulous voice, questioning the opinions, if not the facts, of every speaker. But he was not always in the wrong. Those of you who are of opinion that there is such a thing as meddlesome midwifery, will find support from his remarks made during a discussion on difficult labour cases. "That the less labour was interfered with the better." His own method, however, might not be followed. For he said, if he adopted artificial means at all to expedite the duration of labour, it would be "bleeding and tartar emetic."

Again, in discussing syphilis, he did not approve of any of the recent modes of treatment; he admitted no distinction between the poison of syphilis and that of gonorrhœa, and he advocated "a good mercurial course."

### BARNHILL HOSPITAL, 1852.

The next extract throws an interesting light on the sanitary condition of the Parochial Hospitals in the fifties; and in our mind's eye we can contrast them with the present-day palatial buildings, each with an abundant supply of pure water, and each replete with every recognised invention to ensure perfect sanitation.

In 1852 " Mr Lyon reported, with sorrow, that a very intractable and fatal form of bowel ailment was prevailing at the Parochial Hospital at Barnhill. The disease was not dysentery, the stools were always fecular, there was no absence of bile. It pursued a steady downward progress, sometimes for some weeks, and at length cut off the patient." About fifty cases had occurred, of which number about one-half had proved fatal. Then he says, " With regard to the building, it certainly was not damp ; at the same time it was not clean, intra-mural."

The water-supply was derived from two sunk wells, into one of which it had been discovered that the excrementitious matter from the building had been finding its way. This condition had been put right, but with no apparent effect, as yet, in regard to the extension of the disease. Mr. ¡Menzies considered that the diarrhœa described by Mr. Lyon had its likely origin in the impure water procured from the well referred to. Mr. Menzies " had seen, in tropical climates, diarrhœa produced from sulphuretted hydrogen generated in water containing decomposing vegetable and animal matter, and the disease had given way when the water was changed." The water from the well at Barnhill was subsequently analysed, and Mr. Lyon reported that " it was full of animal matter, the well from which it had been drawn being little better than a diluted sewer ; the sewage of the house had flowed into it." The disease disappeared when the faulty state of the water-supply was rectified.

## CASE OF DISPUTED PATERNITY.

A discussion of considerable medico-legal interest is recorded as having taken place on 16th November, 1852. The president, Dr. James Wilson, mentioned that he had lately been called to a neighbouring village to give evidence in a case of disputed paternity. Twin children had been born seven months after the marriage of the parties, and a practitioner who had been consulted by the husband expressed his belief that they were born at the end of eight months, while another medical man stated his conviction that the twins were seven months' children. With the latter opinion the president had no hesitation in concurring, and he gives very fully the grounds on which he based that opinion.

## EPIDEMIC PHLEGMON.

The presence of phlegmon in an epidemic form is recorded in 1853, due, some thought, to great gastric disturbance, while others thought it to be due to the introduction of a poison into the blood, and that it was contagious. One of the members himself had suffered from it.

## REGISTRATION OF DEATHS ACT, 1855.

That history repeats itself we are reminded by a long and animated discussion in February, 1855, on the new Registration Act as affecting medical men. "While it was agreed that most valuable statistical data would ultimately accrue from the operation of this enactment, the majority of members who took part in the discussion were of opinion that in the penalty attached to the non-fulfilment of what must frequently be a troublesome and in many cases a gratuitous labour, an additional illustration was given of the absence of that consideration due to the profession by those in power." A similar position has, we know, been recently taken up, both by our municipality and the Imperial Parliament, in regard to the compulsory early notification of births.

## MIDWIVES, 1855.

Then bearing on a topic which is meantime a burning question, viz., the necessity for the ensuring of the

fitness of midwives for their duties by the provisions of
the Midwives Bill, I may quote the statement of a
speaker at one of the discussions in 1855 :—" He had been
indirectly concerned with a case where a woman practising as a midwife mistook a prolapsed bladder for protrusion
of the distended membranes, and had actually snipped it
through with a pair of scissors.  A vesico-vaginal fistula
was the result, and the patient died three or four weeks
subsequently.  The same woman, on another occasion,
performed craniotomy by thrusting the identical pair of
scissors into the infant's head; the mother and child
were interred together a few days afterwards."

## INTRA-MURAL INTERMENTS, 1856.

A discussion on intra-mural interments follows a statement bearing on the evidence given by some members in
the " Dumbarton churchyard enquiry."

" Dr. James Adams directed attention to the ' Dumbarton churchyard enquiry' presently pending before
Sheriff Hunter.  The investigation was specially interesting as being the first which had occurred in Scotland,
under the provisions of the recent Parliamentary Act
relative to ' intra-mural interments.'  Among the scientific witnesses, Professors Anderson and Penny, Mr.
Lyon, and himself had given evidence to prove that the
alleged evils of intra-mural interments were greatly
exaggerated—that much popular ignorance prevailed
regarding the subject—and that with reference to the case
of the Dumbarton churchyard no condition dangerous to
the public health existed.

" Numerous witnesses—including the magistrates,
medical men, and clergymen of the town—had alleged
the existence of noxious odours, and dangerous emana-
tions of carbonic acid and sulphuretted hydrogen gas, the
prevalence of epidemic disease, etc., etc.  That these conditions were imaginary had been clearly shown by the
evidence of the witnesses with whom he (Dr. Adams) was

associated. Chemical tests had failed to detect the dele-
terious gases mentioned, and, even if generated, the
state of an open churchyard did not permit of their
accumulation. Dr. Adams, after describing the various
tests which had been employed, admitted that the practice
generally of intra-mural burials had been fearfully abused
—a fact which was abundantly proved by the enquiries
and investigations of a Parliamentary Commission. It
had been shown that in England it was no uncommon circumstance for the number of interments within one acre
of ground to average more than 2,000.''

## SPINA BIFIDA.

To contrast with modern methods and present-day
results, the following case may be quoted:—Dr. Burns, in
1860, showed a specimen of a spina bifida which he had
tapped without success. The tumour was a large cyst,
and contained a small knuckle of the medulla oblongata.
Dr. Lyon had seen many cases of spina bifida, and was
of opinion that the disease always terminated fatally,
and that little benefit was to be derived from treatment
by ligature, by tapping, or by pressure. He considered
that iodine injected within the dura mater would termi-
nate in death.

## EROSION OF THE WALLS OF THE COMMON CAROTID ARTERY.

Two cases are recorded. In one there was a strumous
abscess in the neck, which was opened. Bleeding followed, and to ascertain its source, the wound was extended
and the vessel ligatured. On inspection after death, an
ulcerated opening in the common carotid, communicating
with the sac of the abscess, was found.

## ACTIONS FOR DAMAGES.

At least two cases in which medical men were sued for
damages in the Sheriff Court are recorded in the minutes.

The discussion of each case occupied the whole time of a meeting of the Society.

In January, 1857, Mr. John Reid gave details of "a case which had recently occupied the attention of the medical profession, which had been brought under review in the Sheriff Court, in which a decision had been given affecting much the question of medical privilege." Dr. Reid, as the family medical adviser, had been consulted regarding the condition of the servant maid, and his opinion confirmed the suspicions of the mistress. Several months afterwards an action was raised, and, chiefly on the report of Professor Andrew Buchanan, to whom the pursuer was referred for examination by the Sheriff, and who had "examined the female by all the means known to medical men" with negative results, Dr. Reid "was mulcted in £10 damages and expenses, the Sheriff holding that the plea of medical privilege could not be sustained."

In the second case, a collier in Garnkirk had injured his finger; and a man in Glasgow, "who, it appears, had no legal qualification, and was merely a lad in a druggist's shop," said the finger was fractured, and put it in splints. Ten weeks later, Dr. Oliver, adviser to a local provident society, took the splints off, and gave a line for aliment. A similar application was made seven weeks later, which the doctor refused, and as a result an action for £20 as damages was raised. "The Sheriff-Substitute found the defender liable to seven guineas with expenses." "The Sheriff-Principal adhered, but reduced the damages," holding that Dr. Oliver, by removing the splints, was the cause of "the pursuer being kept off work for a long period, and having been put to much suffering and inconvenience."

## TURKISH BATH.

At the first meeting of session 1860, Dr. G. H. B. Macleod gave what is recorded as "a graphic description of the Turkish bath as employed in the East," and "it

C

was the unanimous opinion of the members present that
while the Turkish bath might, in the majority of cases,
be employed by healthy people in this climate with im-
punity, or even in many instances with advantage to
health, its indiscriminate use, as a medical agent, ought
to be discouraged.''

## INFANTILE MORTALITY.

At the following meeting there was a discussion on
the '' Excessive Infantile Mortality in cities and large
towns.''   Dr. Fraser, who opened the discussion, attributed the excessive death-rate principally to the following special agencies, which he placed in, what appeared
to him, their order of importance :—
1. Overcrowding and vitiated air, imperfect drainage
and deficient supply of light.
2. Deficient nutrition.
3. Want of hospital for sick children.
4. Too early marriages.
5. Neglect of illegitimate children.
All very much as we have it still.

## TOBACCO.

The effects of tobacco, which were discussed at the end
of 1860, and the opinions expressed thereon were as
diverse then as those to which we listen at the present
time.

## SPECIAL HOSPITALS, 1861.

At the meeting of March, 1861, the subject of a hospital
for sick children was introduced and discussed.  The
members present, whilst approving of the classification
of patients for clinical teaching and other purposes in
general hospitals, were almost unanimously of the opinion
that there was no call for the institution of special
hospitals.

In February of the next year the subject of special hospitals and special departments in general hospitals was again introduced, this time by Dr. Andrew Buchanan, jun., who summed up his paper as follows:—

"1. Rational specialism is always good, for there is no subject connected with medical science which will not be more successfully cultivated by men who are constantly studying it, or if an operation, constantly performing it.

"2. The recognition of the principle of specialism in large general hospitals, by placing particular classes of diseases under the care of men, who, while accomplished general physicians, are led by this arrangement to devote their more particular attention to these diseases, tends to promote the advancement of science, renders the labours of the physician more profitable to himself, is better for the purposes of study, and better for the patients, who are thus unquestionably treated in the most satisfactory manner attainable.

"3. Special hospitals on a separate scale are good, provided that the relief afforded them is not disproportionate to the expense of keeping them up."

## TRACHEOTOMY IN DIPHTHERIA.

In a discussion on this subject in 1863, there is evidence of the old order of things passing away. The subject of tracheotomy in croup and diphtheria was introduced by Dr. Reid, who argued that diphtheria was not a new affection, but an old one under a new name. He was strongly opposed to opening the windpipe in croup, and he thought it was seldom required in diphtheria. Dr. Morton thought that death in diphtheria was due to a general poisoning of the blood, such as we saw in scarlet fever, and consequently no good could be got in tracheotomy.

Dr. Lyon looked on croup as an inflammatory, sthenic

complaint to be treated by antiphlogistics, given early and decidedly; and it was only in cases where the local obstruction threatened death that tracheotomy was of any avail. He looked on diphtheria as a totally new disease of which he had had no experience till lately. Dr. A. R. Simpson thought that death in diphtheria was partly due to a poisoning of the blood and partly to a local affection, and in any case in which the latter was present tracheotomy should be performed.

The next remarks are by Professor Gairdner, and are the first made by him of which record is made in those minutes. "He had not seen much of inflammatory croup; he had, however, seen a good many cases of diphtheria lately. In three, tracheotomy had been performed, and all died; still, he thought it was a proper remedy if the cases in which it was put into practice were properly selected."

Dr. Macleod followed. He agreed with Dr. Simpson, and pointed out that it was only in those cases where obstruction was a prominent and threatening sign that tracheotomy could be thought of.

### JESSIE M'LACHLAN.

A paper read by Dr. M'Leod in January, 1863, on the medical evidence in the trial of Jessie M'Lachlan, in which he endeavoured to show that she must have been the person who committed the murder with which she was charged, aroused considerable discussion. The conclusions drawn by the author were freely discussed, and many dissented from the author in various particulars.

### LARYNGOSCOPE.

At the last meeting held in the year 1863, Dr. Forbes read a brief description of the mode of using the laryngoscope, detailing the parts of the larynx which it brings into view. He gave instructions how to use it, and then he proceeded to give an autoscopic demonstration of the various movements occurring in the larynx, which was witnessed, and much esteemed, by the different members present.

### "A MEDICAL STAFF."

Novelties, intended to assist the practitioner in his daily rounds, were brought to the notice of the profession then as now, and as this is the description of one which, I am sure, none of you have seen, I extract the reference to it :—

"Dr. Gray, in 1853, submitted what he called a 'Medical Staff,' the diameter of which did not much exceed that generally carried, and so ingeniously constructed that, when taken to pieces, it was found to contain an enema, catheters, forceps, etc., etc., etc., as well as several of the more potent substances used in medicine." A veritable multum in parvo.

### JOINT MEETINGS.

The Glasgow Medical and the Medico-Chirurgical Societies were throughout on very friendly terms, and worked together harmoniously when occasion called for any joint action.

As has been already noted, the latter Society at its initiation, intimated by a note sent to the President of the Medical Society that the new Society would be happy to admit all the members of the older Society without ballot or any form of election.

In February, 1858, a meeting was held jointly with the Medico-Chirurgical Society for the purpose of seeing M. Groux, of Hamburg. This man had a remarkable congenital deficiency of the sternum, on account of which the motions of the heart could in some measure be exhibited, and Dr. Allen Thomson acted on this occasion as demonstrator.

Again in February, 1863, a joint meeting was held between a committee of the Medical Society, the Faculty, and the Medico-Chirurgical Society on the subject of the regulation of fees.

## PROPOSED AMALGAMATIONS.

At different times proposals for amalgamation with this Society were made by other societies composed of medical men, and amongst those proposals the following are of interest :—

1. The Glasgow Pathological Society, in 1854. The first minute for session 1854-55 opens thus :—" Some conversation followed a proposal made by Dr. Cowan to the effect that an attempt should be made to unite the Glasgow Pathological with this Society, but the matter was allowed to drop."

The Glasgow Pathological Society was formed in 1851. Its meetings were held in the Royal Infirmary, and its members devoted their attention specially to pathological work. Dr. Duncan tells us that " the late Sir William Aitken, and a few other enthusiasts in the field of pathology, threw themselves with energy into the work of this society." The first paper was read, just fifty-six years ago, by Dr. Robert Perry (who is here to-night), the subject of the essay being " The post-mortem appearances in the bladder and ureters in typhus cases." The preparations shown in illustration of his remarks are now in the Pathological Museum of the Royal Infirmary. The Society had a comparatively short life, as it came to an end not long after the proposal of amalgamation above referred to was made.

2. The Medico-Chirurgical Society, in 1860. In October, 1860, Dr. M'Ghie proposed, at a meeting of the Medico-Chirurgical Society (founded in 1844) that " it be remitted to the Council to consider the propriety and expediency of that Society effecting an amalgamation

with the Medical Society," but no record remains of the Medical Society having been approached on the subject.

3. The Medico-Chirurgical Society, in 1863. In November, 1863, Dr. Adams, who was senior secretary to the Medico-Chirurgical Society, and Dr. Reid proposed, at a meeting of the Medical Society, that a committee be appointed to consider the expediency of an amalgamation of this Society with the Medico-Chirurgical Society, chiefly on account of the limited attendance. Drs. Lyon and Smith advocated the continuance of the Medical Society as a distinct Society, and this was approved of by the other members present.

4. The Medico-Chirurgical Society, in 1865. Dr. George H. B. Macleod was elected president of the Glasgow Medical Society in October, 1865, at which date he was junior secretary to the Medico-Chirurgical Society. At the first meeting which he attended after his election to the presidency, it was agreed to discuss the question, " whether it is desirable to amalgamate with the Medico-Chirurgical Society."

The question was discussed in March, 1866, and, as a result, it was unanimously agreed that, " in the opinion of this meeting, the time has now come when it is expedient for this Society to enter into terms of union with the Medico-Chirurgical Society."

" The preses and the secretary of this Society were appointed a committee to confer with any such committee as might be appointed by the Medico-Chirurgical Society, and instructions were given them as to terms, which were that the session of the amalgamated Society should be nine months, the recess being in the months of June, July, and August, with power in the hands of the Council of calling pro re nata meetings when called for."

This amalgamation will be more fully discussed, when the history of the Medico-Chirurgical Society of Glasgow of 1844 is under consideration.

## GLASGOW MEDICO-CHIRURGICAL SOCIETY, CONSTITUTED 1820.

I would here, in parenthesis, make mention of a society which was formed, in 1820, under the name of "The Glasgow Medico-Chirurgical Society."

Dr. Duncan, in describing the medical societies of Glasgow, makes no mention of this one, and, indeed, its very existence seems to have been forgotten until nine years ago. In 1898 Dr. C. Fred. Pollock presented the first minute book of that Society to this Society through Dr. Middleton, our president at that date. Dr. Pollock had received the volume from the grand-daughters of the late Dr. William Lyon, a member of the Society, and probably at one time its secretary, and who also, as we have seen, was a very active member of the Medical Society. A note on this minute book was contributed to the "Glasgow Medical Journal" (November, 1899) by Dr. Middleton. Since the publication of that note the second volume has been recovered, and it, along with its predecessor, is now lodged in the library of the Faculty.

Three medical men—Mr. Marshall, Dr. Ferguson, and Mr. Wilson—met on 13th June, 1820, and, " considering the great advantage which each of them might derive by forming themselves into a Society for the purpose of writing and discussing medical subjects," constituted themselves into a Society.

The Society met twice a month, at first in each other's houses, then for a short time in the College, and, finally, in Cow Pock Hall, St. Andrew's Square.

As in the Medical Society, so here, the reading of papers was compulsory, and fines were exacted for absence, for want of punctuality, etc. At a meeting in 1821 only one member was present, and he, " having waited until his patience was nearly exhausted, it was resolved that all the absentees be fined double." It never was a large Society, and Dr. Middleton tells us that at its fiftieth meeting, there were nine members only, " and the total number who signed the laws was only twenty-one. From this latter list the names of two of the founders are missed ; but on the last page their absence is accounted for, both having absconded." It was essentially an East-End Society, both in regard to its membership and its place of meeting. Bearing on the latter, there is an interesting article in Cleland's " Rise and Progress of the City of Glasgow " which comprises " an account of its Public Buildings, Charities, and Other Concerns." He tells us that a number of medical gentlemen in the city, unconnected with the Faculty of Physicians and Surgeons, formed themselves into a Society for vaccinating the children of the poor, gratis, under the designation of " The Glasgow Cow Pock Institution " ; and that a committee attended in the hall of the institution, St. Andrew's Square, on Fridays, at 12 o'clock, for the purpose of vaccination. It was in this " Cow Pock Hall " that this early Medico-Chirurgical Society held most of its meetings.

I can find no mention in the minute books of either this, or of the Medical Society, of those two associations having had any meetings in common, and there is no indication of amalgamation proposals having been made before the demise of this Medico-Chirurgical Society, which occurred about 1832.

This wellnigh forgotten Society, its personnel and the work which it accomplished, does not therefore concern us further to-night. What the third volume of its minutes might reveal cannot be known until the lost book has been recovered.

## THE MEDICO-CHIRURGICAL SOCIETY OF GLASGOW, FOUNDED IN 1844.

A meeting of medical gentlemen desirous of establishing a Medico-Chirurgical Society in Glasgow took place in Dr. Lawrie's house, 15 Moore Place, on 27th June, 1844. Twenty-six gentlemen were present at the meeting, and other twenty-three, who had been prevented from attending, intimated their wish to become members.

The establishment of the Society was resolved upon at this meeting, and amongst the resolutions agreed upon were, " That there be no compulsory attendance," and " no compulsory reading of papers or communications of any kind." Also that " the Society meet once a month during eight months in the year, commencing in March and ending in October, on the second Tuesday of each month at eight o'clock P.M.," and further, " That the members of the Medical Society of Glasgow be invited to become members, and that the members of the Medico-Chirurgical of Edinburgh, be privileged visitors."

### RELATIONS WITH OTHER SOCIETIES.

Dr. Thomas Thomson, Regius Professor of Chemistry, who had been called to the chair, was elected the first president. At the first ordinary meeting a letter was read from the Medico-Chirurgical Society of Edinburgh, and one from the Medical Society of Glasgow ; and to illustrate the feeling of cordiality which existed then, and continued to exist throughout the years to come, between the Glasgow Medical and the Medico-Chirurgical Societies, I quote the important portion of the letter, which was addressed to the secretary of the Medico-Chirurgical Society, and signed by Dr. Hannay, president of the Medical Society :—

" I am directed by the Society to acknowledge, most

PROFESSOR THOMAS THOMSON.

gratefully, the cordial expression of good feeling towards it by the Medico-Chirurgical Society, so handsomely communicated in your note; and to request the G.M.-C. Society to believe that the Glasgow Medical Society will always rejoice in any good the newly-formed association may be able to accomplish, either in the improvement of its own members, or in the advancement of the healing art in its scientific or practical departments."

It is further recorded at the first meeting that " the Faculty of Physicians and Surgeons had, in reply to the application made, granted the use of the room to this Society in the most handsome manner."

## ITS LAWS.

From the laws we learn that there was no compulsion in the matter of attendance, nor in the reading of papers, and no fines were exacted. " The funds of the Society shall consist," it says, " of an annual contribution of five shillings, to be paid by the ordinary members at the meeting in March, and by new members on the night of their admission." Corresponding and honorary members shall pay no contributions. This Society differed also from the Medical Society in the treatment of the stranger, for it is enacted " that each member shall have the privilege of introducing one medical visitor at every ordinary meeting, who must be provided with the printed admission (form) annexed to the member's billet, on which the visitor's name must be written, and also duly attested by the member's signature." At ordinary meetings " five shall form a quorum, but twelve shall be necessary for the election of members."

At first the ordinary business of the Society consisted in the reading of papers and their subsequent discussion. But in 1852 the Council considered the propriety of holding occasional conversational meetings. It seemed to them expedient that " in the absence of a pressure of important communications, conversational meetings should be held on two or three evenings in the course of each session, and an according discretionary power was committed to the secretaries.

## TRANSACTIONS.

In referring to some of the papers read before the Medico-Chirurgical Society, we may first note that read by Dr. Adam Warden on 8th October, 1844.

## REFLECTING PRISMS, 1844.

The subject was " Reflecting prisms used for illuminating the open cavities of the body, with a view to facilitate the examination of disease and the application of remedial means in such situations." The paper was illustrated by a great variety of " specula " adapted to this method of observation. What parts were thus brought into view is not recorded, and when we remember that this demonstration was given thirteen years before the introduction of the laryngoscope into medicine, the omission is greatly to be regretted. Shortly after this demonstration, Dr. Warden was elected, along with Dr. John Rose Cormack, a corresponding member of the Society.

## SIR JAMES Y. SIMPSON.

In 1845 Dr. J. Y. Simpson, Professor of Midwifery in the University of Edinburgh, was present, and gave a verbal statement of facts regarding the alleged reproduction of part of the superior extremity after amputation in utero ; and in the following year he was again present, and again contributed to the proceedings of the Society.

## CERTIFICATES IN LUNACY.

That the practitioner of medicine encountered difficulties in those days, as they now do, may be gathered from the record of a discussion in 1848, stated shortly in the minutes thus:—" Dr. John Crawford concluded his essay on the difficulties and duties of medical men, in reference to the granting of certificates of insanity, which gave rise to a long and animated discussion."

## INTERESTING EXHIBIT.

In 1849 Dr. Ritchie exhibited a large mass of hair taken from the stomach of a girl who had long been in the habit of swallowing her own hair. It weighed, when extracted, 19 oz., and presented an accurate mould of the organ from which it had been removed.

## INJURY FROM FISH BONE.

Dr. Reid also reported a case in which death had followed penetrating ulceration of the common carotid artery, produced by the end of a fish-bone impacted in the œsophagus.

## DARLINGISM, 1851.

Dr. A. Buchanan read an essay entitled " Darlingism, misnamed Electro-Biology," in which he commented on the recent exhibitions in this city of certain itinerant lecturers on this subject, indicating the points in which their experiments failed to furnish philosophical evidence of the existence of any real influence transmitted from them to the subjects of their experiments, and offering explanations of the phenomena which they appeared to produce, as originating in an excited imagination, or love of notoriety, or a positive intention to deceive on the part of their victims, or, finally, a combination in various proportions of these several causes. A lively discussion ensued, in which the members gave in their unanimous adhesion to the opinions which the essayist had, after careful investigation, expressed.

Following on this discussion it was unanimously agreed

—" That the Society deems it to be its duty to endeavour to put down a system founded on delusion, and fraught with immorality, and, thinking this address well fitted to promote that important end, resolves that the same be published at the expense of the Society."

## PLAGIARISM, 1852.

In 1852 much excitement in the Society was occasioned by a charge of plagiarism, preferred against one of its members. This gentleman had read a paper at the Philosophical Society entitled " On the Occurrence of Sugar in the Animal Economy," and in which he was said to have arrogated to himself the credit of M. Bernard's discoveries with respect to the existence and mode of production of sugar in the animal body. " To understand the grounds of the accusation, it is necessary to bear in mind that the paper was not published in a medical journal, to be read by medical men, upon whom such an imposition could not easily have been practised, but was published as part of the proceedings of a society, the great proportion of whose members are quite unacquainted with physiological subjects."

Much correspondence between the Council, the accused, and others, followed the receipt of the accusation. The Council examined the paper as published in the Transactions of the Philosophical Society, with the result that " the Council is of opinion that the charge of plagiarism admits of being fully established," and the particulars of the grounds are stated in its minutes. One point is interesting as being specially condemnatory. " So literal is the translation which he gives of one of the most important of Bernard's experiments on this subject, that he completely perverts the meaning of the author by translating literally an error of the press. This it is scarcely possible he could have done, had he really repeated, as he claims to have done, the experiments of Bernard. He therefore here lays himself open to a charge far more serious than that of plagiarism—that of representing himself to have performed experiments which he never performed."

The report drawn up by the Council was read at the meeting in October, when the following motion was adopted:—"That the Society, having heard the report of the Council, and being now enabled to judge of the nature of the offence charged against" the member, "are of opinion that it can only be viewed as a moral offence; that the said offence was not committed against this Society; and that the Society is in no way implicated thereby. They are further of opinion that this Society was instituted solely for the promotion of medical science and literature, and has never pretended to exercise a moral censorship over its members, and would infallibly involve itself in innumerable difficulties by attempting to do so; and the Society therefore resolves that it is inexpedient to proceed further in this matter, and that the report be not inserted in the minutes."

## A GRIEVANCE.

Attention was called on 13th April, 1852, to the discreditable fashion in which the names of members of the profession are ranked with those of unqualified and irregular practitioners in the list purporting to be of physicians and surgeons, published in the Glasgow Post Office Directory. The Society generally expressed their sense of the grievance, and their obligation to Dr. Thomson for moving in the matter. As, however, they have no coercive power, they resolved to memorialise the Faculty of Physicians and Surgeons as to the exercise of their statutory authority over irregular practitioners within their bounds.

### ECHO OF IMPORTANT EVENTS.

Important events in the history of our country, in the criminal history of our city, and in the history of surgery, are recalled by many of the subjects discussed.

### THE CRIMEA.

In June, 1857, Dr. George Buchanan read an interesting communication from Dr. William Aitken " On the Medical History of the War with Russia—the Influence of the Residence in Bulgaria on the Health of the Army in the Crimea."

### MARRIAGE OF PRINCE OF WALES.

At a Council meeting in February, 1863, it was agreed to hold the first meeting of the session about to begin on Wednesday, 11th March, as the regular night of meeting, viz., 10th March, had been appointed a general holiday on account of the marriage of the Prince of Wales.

### MADELINE SMITH.

At the July meeting in 1857 the evening was occupied in professional conversation, which turned principally on interesting points connected with, or suggested by, the recent protracted trial of Miss Madeline Smith for the suspected murder by poison of M. L'Angelier.

### DR. PRITCHARD.

We have, in the minutes of meeting held in July, 1865, an echo of the trial of Dr. Pritchard of this city, for poisoning his wife and mother-in-law, by " the report of experiments made by Dr. Adams and Dr. Penny, made with the view of determining by a physiological test the presence of aconite in a suspected fluid."

## OVARIOTOMY.

Dr. George Buchanan described a successful case of ovariotomy at the meeting held on 14th June, 1864, and he was complimented on the success of his case, which was stated, and acknowledged to be, the first successful case of ovariotomy in the West of Scotland.

## VISIT OF THE BRITISH ASSOCIATION.

In September, 1860, it was remitted to the Council " to consider the expediency of holding, and, if approved of, to make the necessary arrangements for a conversazione of the Society, to take place during the meetings in Glasgow of the British Association for the promotion of Social Science."

## PROPOSED CHANGE IN DATE OF MEETING.

In October, 1860, on the motion of Dr. Adams, it was remitted to the Council with full powers to select some other evening than Tuesday for holding the meetings of the Society, which motion was seconded by Dr. Lyon and agreed to.

## PROPOSED AMALGAMATION, 1860.

At the same meeting, on the motion of Dr. M'Ghie, " it was remitted to the Council to consider the propriety and expediency of this Society effecting an amalgamation with the Medical Society."

## A BLANK IN THE COUNCIL MINUTE BOOK.

The minutes containing those three separate remits end with the words " vide minutes of Council." But on referring to the minute book of the Council, to ascertain the fate of those recommendations, a series of blank pages is encountered—there is, in fact, no record of the doings of the Council between 29th March, 1860, and 22nd May,

1862. Whether the conversazione to the members of the British Association was ever held or not, is not recorded, and whether the Medical Society was approached on this occasion with a view to amalgamation is not noted.

Further, a search of the minute book of the Medical Society reveals no statement on the subject of amalgamation, or the holding of any conference between the members or Council of the two Societies on this subject at this time.

### DEARTH OF MATERIAL.

In July, 1860, while meetings were held regularly, there must have been difficulty in obtaining a sufficient supply of material for those meetings, for in July it is recorded that " the Society take into consideration a recommendation from the Council in regard to the propriety of adopting a compulsory or some such system in the reading of papers or communications." After some discussion, and without coming to a vote, it was resolved that the proposal of the Council should not in the meantime be carried out.

### LARYNGOSCOPE.

Dr. W. B. Mackinlay exhibited a laryngoscope at the first meeting in 1861, and described the method of its employment.

### CANCRUM ORIS.

In 1862, what is described as an interesting paper on cancrum oris was read, in which the author endeavoured to establish a causal connection between deficiency of sulphur in the blood and the existence of this disease.

### "GLASGOW MEDICAL JOURNAL."

Many references to the " Glasgow Medical Journal " are met with throughout the minutes of this Society. Objections are sometimes raised on account of the un-authorised publication of papers read at the meetings, at other times the question at issue is regarding the reporting of the proceedings, but the difficulties and differences discussed are, for the most part, of a financial character.

On 9th March, 1852, the statement of accounts, as laid before the Society by the treasurer, showed a balance in his hands of £34, 4s. 6d. A conversation followed this statement on the expediency of the Society applying its surplus funds to, or otherwise interesting itself in, the establishment and support of a medical journal for Glasgow and the West of Scotland, and a committee was appointed to inquire into ways and means.

The Committee reported at the next meeting that an octavo journal of six sheets might be published at an expense not exceeding £20 per number for 500 copies, but they desired time to make further enquiries.

In October of the same year Dr. Andrew Buchanan urged on the profession the establishment of a medical journal for the West of Scotland, and Dr. Pagan, at the same meeting, expressed his willingness to place his paper in the hands of the conductors, for publication in the first number.

The final recommendation is made at the meeting held on 28th November, 1853, the words of the motion being, " That whereas the proprietors of the ' Glasgow Medical Journal ' have laid before the Council a scheme whereby its publication shall be continued for at least two years from January, 1854, and whereby three delegates from the Council of this Society shall be added to the body having the conduct of the work, the Council agrees to recommend to the Society a grant of fifty pounds from its funds, provided that the said scheme be carried into effect."

In April, 1865, it was agreed that, in consideration of the expense incurred by the proprietors of the " Glasgow Medical Journal " in the recording of medical intelligence, there should be presented to the editors of the " Journal " the sum of one guinea for each night on which the Society holds a meeting.

### ORDINARY MEETINGS.

The ordinary meetings were held on the second Tuesday of each month, beginning in March and ending in October, at eight o'clock.

The many suggestions which are found to have been made and recorded in the minutes with the view of changing the day and hour of meeting, as also the season, illustrates the difficulty of having a fixed day and hour of meeting which will suit or satisfy every member of a fairlv large Society.

### HOUR OF MEETING.

In April, 1855, it was intimated that some of the country members had represented to the Council that the lateness of the present hour of meeting prevents their attendance, except under the inconvenience of passing the night in town. So at the following meeting it was unanimously resolved that the meetings of the Society shall in future be held at seven o'clock instead of eight o'clock P.M.

Five months later attention was called to the scanty attendance of country members, and it was proposed that it be remitted to the Council to consider the propriety of reverting to the former hour of meeting, and, if it should seem desirable, to carry the change into effect at the beginning of next session. The Society, however, were of opinion that the present experiment should be continued for a little longer.

Frequently throughout the following session motions were tabled that the Society re-adopt eight o'clock as their hour of meeting, without any change being effected, and seven o'clock continued to be the hour of meeting for ten years.

### WINTER SESSION PROPOSED.

In September, 1863, it was remitted to the Council to make inquiries regarding the propriety of extending the meetings of the Society into the winter, and of making such other alterations as to the duration of the session and the hours of meeting as may extend the usefulness of the Society.

Although this was unanimously agreed to, no note of it occurs in the minutes of the Council, and no action was taken. Each session continued as before to begin in March and close in October until 1866.

At the opening meeting of session 1865, two proposals emanating from the Council were discussed. The first was that a reporter should be employed to attend the meetings of the Society, and this was referred to a committee to make arrangements with the editor of the "Journal." And the second motion was that the hour of meeting should be changed to eight o'clock. In favour of this change, it was argued that this was the original hour of meeting, and that seven o'clock had been substituted for it in the hope of inducing the country members to attend, but the experience of the last two sessions had proved that hope to be groundless. Secondly, eight o'clock was a much more convenient hour than seven for town members. This proposal was almost unanimously agreed to, and the hour of meeting was altered accordingly.

### FACULTY REMOVAL.

In 1862 the Faculty removed from St. Enoch's Square to its present premises. While the hall was being put in order the Society met first at 21 Blythswood Square, then at 115 West Campbell Street, and it did not again meet in the Faculty Hall until the opening of its twentieth session in March, 1863.

### FUNDS.

At the close of the first financial year the treasurer had a balance in hand in favour of the Society of £6, 3s. 7d.; but one year later, the committee appointed to examine the state of the treasurer's books reported that they had compared the various vouchers and found remaining in the hands of the treasurer the sum of fourpence, and that the arrears of annual contributions amounted to £2, 10s. The sensation of novelty had passed, and the duty of each member to the treasurer and the Society had apparently been forgotten.

### OFFICER.

In October, 1849, the treasurer was instructed " to pay seven pounds in equal portions to Rice Jones and John Menzies ; to intimate to the former that his services would not again be required ; and to fix the salary of the latter at two guineas for each session."

This curt intimation to Mr. Rice Jones, who acted as officer to this, as well as to the Medical Society, lacks the human note which pervades the minutes of the latter Society, and which I have already quoted, touching the frailties which rendered him unfit for further duty.

At this same meeting the secretaries were instructed to henceforth send all billets of intimation by post, and to discontinue the supply of coffee at ordinary meetings.

### REPAYMENT OF SUBSCRIPTION.

In 1850 a letter was read from Dr. Wylie requesting repayment of his subscription for last session on the ground that he was elected at the penultimate meeting, and was unable to be present at the final one. The Council instructed the treasurer to pay the amount, and recommended that " in future no subscription for the current session be exacted from any gentleman who shall become a member of the Society after the sixth meeting." As there were seven meetings only in the session, this was no very great concession.

### DISPOSAL OF FUNDS.

In 1853 the treasurer had a balance of £44, 3s. 5d. in hand. Mr. Reid, having reference to the present state of the funds, proposed that after a certain number of years, members should cease to pay annual contributions. This being considered private business, was remitted to the Council. At the subsequent meeting of Council, it was proposed, though not by the treasurer, that after payments amounting in the aggregate to two pounds, no member should henceforth be called on for an annual contribution, unless the accumulated fund should fall below fifty pounds. This proposal, however, was negatived by a majority.

Again, in 1858, a discussion on the propriety of reducing the annual subscription after the first year of membership to 2s. 6d., or, alternatively, the adoption of a scheme by which members should have the power of commuting their annual payments for a definite sum paid on entry. The subject was remitted to the Council, who, after consideration of the remit, agreed to recommend that the annual subscription should be continued unchanged.

### GUARANTEED £25—BROWN SEQUARD'S LECTURES.

In 1859 Dr. George M'Leod approached the Council to assist financially a scheme which he had taken much trouble in promoting, viz., to invite Dr. Brown Sequard to deliver a course of lectures in Glasgow. The course had been arranged for, but subscribers at one guinea each, sufficient to produce fifty pounds, the minimum amount which could be offered to the lecturer, had not been forthcoming, and Dr. M'Leod requested a grant of a sum not exceeding twenty-five pounds, which would secure the delivery of the lectures at a fee not exceeding half-a-guinea. The Council agreed to supplement any deficiency in the subscriptions, not exceeding twenty-five pounds.

These lectures were most successful. '' A note from Dr.

George M'Leod informed the Society that the number of subscribers to the lectures of Dr. Brown Sequard had been so great that no call on the funds of the Society, in terms of their guarantee, would be requisite."

## SUBSCRIBED £10, 10s. TO THE JOHN HUNTER STATUE.

Four months later the Society voted unanimously a sum of ten guineas to the fund for the erection in London of a statue in honour of John Hunter.

## £20 TOWARDS REPEAL OF PENALTY CLAUSE IN THE REGISTRATION BILL.

In April, 1861, it was agreed that twenty pounds of the Society's funds be set aside to assist the movement for procuring a repeal of the penalty system, as applied to Scotland, for obtaining certificates of the cause of death. And, further, that the treasurer be instructed to hand over the above-named sum to Dr M'Carron, the treasurer of the Faculty of Medicine. This was done, but nothing came of the agitation.

## PROVIDING TEA AND COFFEE.

In the Medical Society, the admission of strangers to the meetings, as I have already indicated, formed the subject of frequent discussion. The favourite theme with the Medico-Chirurgical Society, as recorded in the transactions of the Council, appears to have been that of providing tea and coffee at the ordinary meetings.

At the first meeting of the Council of the Society, in June, 1844, " it was unanimously agreed that coffee should be served at the termination of every ordinary meeting, in conformity with the practice followed by the various literary and scientific institutions of London and Edinburgh."

In 1849, however, funds were low, and the secretaries were instructed regarding various economies, and, amongst

them, " to discontinue the supply of coffee at the ordinary
meetings."

## CONVERSAZIONE.

The opening meeting of session 1859 " took the form of
a conversational meeting, when a large number of the
members and their friends attended.    After tea and coffee,
which was supplied in the reading-room, the company proceeded to the Hall, where casts, drawings, new instru-
ments, and microscopic objects of interest were submitted
for their inspection, after which the Society proceeded to
the ordinary business."

## STOP TEA AND COFFEE, 1862.

In 1862 it was unanimously agreed that the supply of
tea and coffee at the ordinary meetings of the Society
should be discontinued.    This resolution was determined,
I presume, by the receipt of " an account of £11, 5s. for
refreshments supplied at the opening meeting of the
session."    This account was remitted to two members of
Council, with instructions to settle the claim, " after representing that the same was a heavy over-charge."

But this extravagance was soon forgotten, for we find
two years later the Council again recommending that " tea
and coffee be provided on the first night of the session."

The Society in 1865 had £60, 7s. 9d. to its credit, and I
assume the possession of this wealth was the reason for the
following    resolution :—" It    was    agreed    that    at    the
Society's meetings during the session there should be provided tea and coffee from half-past seven till eight o'clock,
and the secretaries were instructed to intimate the same
on the billets."

But early in March of the following year we find the
secretary suggesting " that refreshments at the Society's
meetings might be purveyed more economically than at
present, by resuming certain arrangements that at one

time were in use, and it was remitted to the secretary to make such arrangements if practicable."

## THE RESOURCEFUL SECRETARY.

Dr. Adams, whom I have already referred to as an efficient secretary of the Medical Society, was elected secretary of the Medico-Chirurgical Society, along with Dr. G. H. B. Macleod, in 1862. Here he was quite as efficient, and perhaps more energetic, as may be illustrated by his action in March, 1866. At a meeting of Council he read a letter, which he had received the previous evening from Dr. Fleming, whom the Council had agreed to nominate for the office of president. Dr. Fleming, in the letter, stated that " while he highly appreciated the intended compliment, he regretted much that at present his engagements would preclude his accepting, or performing, the duties of the office, if elected, and he therefore requested that his name should be withdrawn before the election."

The letter had been delivered at a late hour, and " no sufficient time had since intervened to admit of a meeting of Council, and of any action following such meeting, by which the contingency might be met. Dr. Adams had therefore taken it upon himself to wait upon Dr. Allen Thomson, and request his permission to allow himself to be nominated for the office of president, to which Dr. Thomson had very kindly consented." This prompt action was rewarded, for " the Council very cordially approved, and commended the action taken by Dr. Adams, and agreed that Dr. Thomson's name should be proposed as president in the name of the Council." This action of the secretary was the means by which Dr. Allen Thomson had the honour of becoming the first president of the amalgamated Society.

## PROPOSED AMALGAMATION, 1865.

At the first meeting of the twenty-second session, held on 14th March, 1865, Dr. Ritchie, in his presidential address, spoke of the advantages of such associations to medical men.   He then made various suggestions as to amalgamation of the Medical and the Medico-Chirurgical Societies, the obtaining of a Royal Charter for the united association, and suggested that committees should be appointed to report to the Society, from time to time, anything occurring in the various departments assigned to them worthy of the Society's attention, or to prosecute original research on any special point.

At the meeting of the Council in the following month (April, 1865), the various suggestions contained in the address delivered by Dr. Ritchie, on the first meeting of the session, were considered.   The Council highly approved of that recommendation which related to the amalgamation of the Glasgow Medical with the Medico-Chirurgical Society, and were unanimous in opinion that such union would tend greatly to the prosperity and successful action of the united Society.   The subject, however, was not brought before the notice of the Society until the first meeting of the next session, 13th March, 1866, when the minute of the Council above referred to was read, accompanied by the statement that the Council strongly recommended the subject for the favourable consideration of the Society.

The Society approved the report of the Council, and remitted it back with instructions to hold a conference with the Glasgow Medical Society, and to bring up a report on the arrangements by which the proposed amalgamation should be carried into effect.

## AMALGAMATION WITH THE MEDICAL SOCIETY CONCLUDED, 1866.

In accordance with the remits from the Glasgow Medical and the Medico-Chirurgical Societies, a meeting of representatives of the former with the Council of the latter was held on 27th April, 1866, and, after careful consideration, the conjoint committees agreed to recommend—

" 1. That on and after 12th June of the present year the Glasgow Medical and the Glasgow Medico-Chirurgical Societies should form a united Society under the name of the Glasgow Medico-Chirurgical Society, the existing property of both Societies becoming the property of the new Society, and the members of both Societies becoming, by the act of union, members of the newly constituted Society, and having an equal interest in its property and privileges.

" 2. That the ordinary meetings of the Society should be held on the first Tuesday of each month, commencing in September and ending in May, thus constituting a session of nine months; and that extra meetings should be held on the third Tuesday of the same month as often as in the judgment of the president and secretaries it may be judged desirable.

" 3. That the first meeting of the Society, as anew constituted, should be held on the first Tuesday in September, 1866, on which date the election of office-bearers for the session 1866-67 should take place."

The further recommendations are concerned with the office-bearers and the length of time they should hold office, with members presently in arrears, and with the preparation of a list of members and a set of rules.

The report of the conjoint committee containing the above recommendations was read at a meeting of the Medico-Chirurgical Society on 8th May, 1866. It was approved, and it was again remitted to the same conjoint committee to consider the details of arrangement connected with the amalgamation and future management of the conjoint Society.

Accordingly, the committee again met and discussed the arrangements requisite under the new constitution of the amalgamated Societies, and agreed—

" 1. That the first meeting of the Society for the session 1866-67 should be summoned for Tuesday, 4th September, 1866.

" 2. That the list of office-bearers, as elected in March, 1866, should be recommended for re-election, with the addition of two members of Council, viz., Dr. M'Leod and Dr. A. R. Simpson.

" 3. That no subscription should be exigible for the session 1866-67, commencing 4th September.

" 4. That the salary of the officer be augmented to £5 annually.

" 5. That the Society date its institution from the year 1814."

### LAST MEETING OF THE OLD MEDICO-CHIRURGICAL SOCIETY.

At the end of the twenty-third session, i.e., on 26th June, 1866, the chairman intimated at the close of the meeting that this was the last meeting of the Medico-Chirurgical Society, and that the first meeting of the new Medico-Chirurgical Society, as constituted by the union of the Glasgow Medical Society and the Medico-Chirurgical Society of Glasgow, would be held in September for election of office-bearers and other business.

### THE UNION.

The two Societies had been in no sense of the term rivals, many practitioners were members of both, but in recent years they had been doing similar work on identical lines. It was therefore supposed that united action would probably lead to a wider interest in the work, to greater efficiency in its performance, and to an increase in the attendance at the meetings.

On more than one occasion have I heard it said that our Society originated in 1844, and that it has no ground for claiming 1814 as the date of its institution, but the reverse is the case.

The proposal originated with the younger Society, which, when the details were arranged, was absorbed by the older Society. That this is so, is shown by the fact that the work of the united Society was begun as if it was simply a continuation of the Medical Society.

The first session began in September and ended in May —which constituted the session of the Medical Society since 1816—and the day and hour of meeting determined upon, were those of the Medical Society. It is true that the name of the younger Society was adopted; possibly a spirit of tolerance towards the surgeon had come over the older members of the Medical Society. But be that as it may, had the change of title not been made then, it would have certainly been demanded now, for the greater part of our present-day proceedings relate to surgery and surgical procedure, and if the title was to be changed to-day, possibly the surgeon would demand first place in the superscription. It was a right and proper move to recognise by name the two great branches of the healing art in naming the amalgamated Society.

Another fact bearing on this subject is that our treasurer, even to this day, records his transactions with the funds of this Society, in the self-same book which was used by the first treasurer of the Medical Society at, and from, its foundation in 1814.

It may be interesting here to note the names and the official position of the two gentlemen who were most active in urging the advantages of amalgamation.

First, there was Dr. James Adams, who had been secretary of the Medical Society from 1846 to 1852. He was president of the Medical Society for session 1862-63, at which date he was also the senior secretary of the Medico-Chirurgical Society. It was he who, in November, 1863, while president of the one and secretary of the other Society, proposed that the Medical Society should appoint a committee " to consider the expediency of an amalgamation of the two Societies," which, however, came to nothing.

Secondly, when the question was placed before the Medical Society in 1865, viz., " whether it is desirable to amalgamate with the Medico-Chirurgical Society," it was put by Dr. G. H. B. Macleod, the newly-elected president of the Medical Society, and who, up till the time of his election to this office, had been the junior secretary of the Medico-Chirurgical Society.

The phraseology employed in describing the various steps taken towards the amalgamation, is certainly not that of the lawyer. It is inexact, and " whereas " is conspicuous by its absence ; but notwithstanding the use of the word " old " applied to the Medico-Chirurgical Society formed in 1844, and the word " new " applied once or twice to the Medico-Chirurgical Society subsequent to amalgamation, all doubt in regard to the feelings and intentions of those who brought about the union is dispelled by the fact that the committees appointed by the two amalgamating Societies placed on record, as one of the conditions on which amalgamation should take place, " that the Society should date its institution from the year 1814." (Minute of Society, 4th September, 1866.)

## AMALGAMATION, 1866.

The first meeting of the Society as constituted anew by the amalgamation of the Glasgow Medical and Medico-Chirurgical Societies was held on the evening of Tuesday, 4th September, 1866, under the presidency of Dr. Allen Thomson, who was on that evening elected president for the ensuing session.   Minutes of the Council, dated 14th August, were read and approved, in which, inter alia, it was recommended that " no subscription should be exigible for session 1866-67 ; that the salary of the officer should be augmented to five pounds annually ; and that the Society should date its institution from the year 1814."

### PRESIDENT'S ADDRESS.

" Dr. Thomson addressed the Society in remarks appropriate to the objects of the Association, making special reference to the peculiar circumstances of the meeting as constituted that evening."

### TRANSACTIONS.

Many important communications have been submitted to this Society since the amalgamation took place.   Of these I shall refer to a few only, and that in a few words.

### LORD LISTER, 1868.

In the minutes under date 17th April, 1868, we find the record of a very important meeting—important whether it be viewed in relation to its influence on the surgery of to-day, or from an historical standpoint.   And as this was, perhaps, the first occasion on which Lord Lister publicly described the results of his investigations on the treatment of wounds with antiseptic dressings, I quote the minute in full.

PROFESSOR ALLEN THOMSON.

" An extra meeting of the Society was held to-night, and the president occupied the chair.

" Mr Lister gave a lengthened exposition of the atmospheric germ theory of putrefaction, and illustrated it by the exhibition of M. Pasteur's experiment with flasks containing urine.

" He next directed attention to the employment of carbolic acid for the destruction of the germs presumed to exist in the air, and which Mr. Lister supposed to be the exciting cause of putrefaction in wounds ; and he gave the details of a case in which a young man sustained an incised wound of the left side of the thorax, with penetration through the diaphragm, and protrusion of the omentum through the wound externally.  The protruding portion of omentum was cut off; and although the left pleural cavity was so distended with air and hæmorrhage as to cause displacement of the heart to the right side of the chest, the young man made a perfect recovery under the carbolic acid dressing.

" Mr. Lister next described the effects of a ligature applied, on the antiseptic system, to the carotid of a horse, and showed the portion of the artery and the superjacent skin, as well as the ligature, all of which had been removed from the horse, which had died, from some disease unconnected with the operation, thirteen days after.

" He also narrated a case of ligature of the external iliac artery by the same method, and the history of a case of necrosis of the tibia, in which none of the dead bone had come away, but was presumed to have been absorbed.

" The mode of dressing wounds with carbolic acid was next described—one part of carbolic acid in twenty of water being recommended for an internal application, and for an external dressing, after experimenting with a number of different substances, Mr. Lister had arrived at the conclusion that emplastrum plumbi, with a fourth of its weight of beeswax, and impregnated with carbolic acid, is the most suitable.  The strength of the dressing ought,

E

however, in all cases to be regulated by the nature of the wound.

A discussion following was, chiefly owing to the late hour, confined principally to the cause of putrefaction in wounds, and the theory which had been advanced by Mr. Lister to account for the antiseptic properties of the carbolic acid."

This demonstration given by Lord Lister at this Society in April, 1868, proves, if proof were necessary, that his investigations into the antiseptic treatment of wounds was not only begun in Glasgow, but even then had been so successfully employed by him in the wards of the Glasgow Royal Infirmary, that he was able to demonstrate the satisfactory results he had obtained in this very room. For twelve months longer, he remained Professor of Surgery in Glasgow, and one of the surgeons to the Royal Infirmary.

His communication was followed by at least two papers antagonistic to what was spoken of later, as "Listerism." One of these was by Dr. Eben. Watson, "On the theory of suppuration and the use of carbolic acid dressings," in which he cast doubt on the presence of germs in the air and their alleged association with the formation of pus. The second was by Dr. Morton, "On carbolic acid—its therapeutic position—with special reference to its use in severe surgical cases." From experience, he had "come to the conclusion that it was not superior, and in many cases it was inferior, to other methods of treatment."

These papers notwithstanding, the antiseptic treatment of wounds was adopted by many even in those early days. In January, 1873, Dr. Alex. Patterson read "Notes on five weeks' practice of surgery in the Glasgow Royal Infirmary," and in the minutes we find "the essayist referred to the antiseptic mode of treatment which had been carried out in those cases, and he spoke of it in the highest possible terms, ranking it only second to chloroform, as a boon to practical surgery."

## SEWAGE.

In 1868 also the sewage question, and the purification of the river, bulk largely in the transactions.

## URARA POISON.

In March, 1871, Dr. Dougall read a paper on the urara poison, in which he gave an outline of the history of its discovery and its method of preparation. He also detailed shortly the result of some experiments which he had made with it upon animals. He exhibited a number of the poisoned arrows, and the bamboo tube used by the Indians for projecting them. Attempts were made to poison a rabbit, a fowl, and a pigeon by the insertion of arrows beneath the skin, but they all unaccountably failed.

## LORD KELVIN.

Sir William Thomson gave a lecture " On the diffusion of liquids and gases,'' illustrated by experiments to show the extreme slowness of the diffusion of liquids on the one hand, and the great rapidity of the diffusion of gases on the other.

## ANÆSTHETICS, 1890 AND 1902.

An important discussion, and one which aroused much interest, was that on anæthetics held in October, 1890. It was opened by the president, Dr. William Macewen, in a most interesting paper, and the whole discussion, edited by the secretary, was published in pamphlet form in 1891. The same topic was again the subject of discussion, and practically by another generation, in December, 1902, as most of you interested in the subject will remember.

## TUBERCULOSIS, 1891 AND 1901.

A discussion, which led to important results, on " Tuberculosis as an infectious disease,'' was introduced by Dr. Lindsay Steven on 18th December, 1891. Professor Gairdner, who took part, considered the question a much larger one than the previous speakers had indicated. He was in the habit of teaching that tubercle is the one disease where infectiousness had been accurately proved, and the logical issue of this is that we should isolate our tubercular patients as lepers were isolated. But that he was not prepared to face at present. He moved, "That a memorial be presented to the Town Council of Glasgow, calling their attention to the fact that tuberculosis is now fully recognised as an infectious disease, and asking them to take the matter into their serious consideration with a view to the protection of the community from the infection." This motion was carried, and a deputation was subsequently received by the magistrates in the City Chambers.

Eight years later, as you all know, this Society took an active part in the establishment of a Branch in Glasgow of the National Association for the Prevention of Tuberculosis.

Again, in 1901, an important discussion on the "Provisions for the treatment and relief of the tuberculous poor" was held. It was opened by Professor M'Call Anderson, Dr. Lindsay Steven, and Dr. A. K. Chalmers. Some members of the Town Council were present, and took part in the discussion, by invitation.

### NEW MIDWIVES BILL, 1890.

At a meeting of Council held in October, 1890, the secretary read a communication which had been received from Dr. Rintoul, of Liverpool, containing several suggested resolutions opposed to the proposed "New Midwives Bill." The letter was discussed, and Professor Gairdner expressed the opinion "that the discussion of subjects in medical politics was foreign to the objects of the Society." As this opinion was acquiesced in by those

present, it was agreed " That this Council do not think
that the subject should be discussed by this Society, but
think that the communication be read to the Society, in
whose hands it may be left."

## DR. PAVY.

In January, 1896, Dr. F. W. Pavy of London gave an
interesting address on some points connected with the
pathology and treatment of diabetes mellitus.    The
address was delivered in the hall of the Philosophical
Society, and was listened to by a large audience of practitioners and students.

## OFFICE-BEARERS.

In the Glasgow Medical Society, the office-bearers consisted of the president, two vice-presidents, a treasurer,
and a secretary, and the business of the Society was conducted by the Society itself.    For special business a committee was occasionally appointed, but there was no
Council, so the story of the Society and its doings is contained in the minutes of the ordinary meetings.

The Medico-Chirurgical Society, on the other hand, had
an elected Council, consisting of a president, two vice-
presidents, a treasurer, and two secretaries, together with
six other members ; and this Council regulated the private
business of the Society.  But the ruling of the Council
has not always given satisfaction.

## ELECTION OF OFFICE-BEARERS.

The law on the subject of election of office-bearers was
" That the Council shall regulate the private business of
the Society," and thus we find in an early minute of the
Council, " It was agreed that, in accordance with the laws
of the Society, the Council should recommend the following gentlemen as office-bearers in room of those whose

tenure of office terminates at this date," and later, " The vacant offices were filled up in accordance with the recommendations of the Council."

In 1848 Dr. Morton moved that " in future the office-bearers of this Society be elected by ballot, without any recommendation from the Council." Suspicion of the Council and its motives is a chronic ailment, and one which is not confined to medical societies. In our own time many difficulties have cropped up, and when least expected. When the Council, as a Council, took no part in the election of office-bearers, members were frequently proposed at the meeting, at which proposals were received, who either did not desire to hold office, or who, on account of other engagements or residence at a considerable distance, found it impossible to attend the meetings of the Council. The result was great difficulty in getting a quorum when a meeting of Council was called. So much was this felt that at a meeting of this Society held on 22nd May, 1886, the following recommendation was made and agreed to :—" That the sederunt be taken at each meeting, and that the Council take into account the attendance of members in nominating a certain number for election as office-bearers and Council of the Society," and also, " that a leet of twenty be annually so nominated."

The leet so chosen is entered in the minutes of the Council for September, 1886, but it was not further put into practice ; and at next meeting of Council, which was held at the close of an adjourned meeting of the Society (called specially to consider the better working of the Society, election of office-bearers, institution of sectional meetings, etc.), it was resolved that the election of office-bearers be left entirely in the hands of the Society. There it remains to this day, and the wish of the president and Council is that the members take such interest in the Society as to make their nominations in good time, and nominate members who will devote some time to the duties of their offices.

### DAYS AND HOUR OF MEETING BEFORE AMALGAMATION.

Prior to amalgamation both societies had fixed upon Tuesday as their day of meeting, and it remained so with each until they united. The Medical Society met on the first and third Tuesday of each month from September till May, while the Medico-Chirurgical Society met on the second Tuesday of each month from March till October.

### AFTER AMALGAMATION.

At the first meeting of the re-organised Society it was proposed by Dr. Steven "that the ordinary meetings of the Society shall be held on the first Friday of each month during the session." This motion was considered at the next meeting. It was the cause of a considerable amount of discussion and the movement of amendments, but when put to the vote the motion was declared to be carried by a majority, and the Society resolved accordingly. From that date till now, the first Friday of the month has remained the statutory day of meeting. But although it has remained so, there have been attempts to have it altered. The last attempt was made by Professor George Buchanan when he was president in 1880. He proposed Monday in place of Friday as the day of meeting, but, when it was discussed at the Council, it was generally agreed that Monday was not a convenient evening for the majority of the members, and the president withdrew his motion.

In like manner it is as difficult to fix upon an hour, as it is on a day, which will suit, equally, the convenience of every member of a large Society like this.

Eight o'clock remained the hour of meeting from the date of amalgamation in 1866 till 1886, when, on account of the small number of members who attended the ordinary meetings, it was resolved after discussion that the

night of meeting remain the same, viz., the first Friday
of the month, but that the hour be later, viz., 8.30, in
place of 8 o'clock, as formerly.

In 1891 it was again proposed that the hour of meeting
should be 8 P.M., but the proposal was negatived.

## SECTIONS, 1886.

With the object of further increasing the interest of
the profession in the work of the Society, it was arranged
in 1886 that the work should be done in sections, and
the Society was accordingly divided into four sections
—Medicine, Surgery, Pathology, and Obstetrics—each
section having a vice-president, two councillors, and a
secretary.

For a time, increased interest was shown, and then not
only did the attendance fall off, but those members, presumably specially interested in the work of a particular
section, were, at the meetings of that section, frequently
conspicuous by their absence.  So, in 1894, it was agreed
that while the sections would be retained, individual
meetings should not be confined to the subject of any one
section, but that there should be "mixed billets," to give
greater general interest to the proceedings.

While sections are still retained nominally, they are
shorn of their importance in having no vice-president and
no sectional secretary.

## PUBLICATION OF THE TRANSACTIONS OF THE SOCIETY.

Although the proceedings of the Society had appeared
regularly for many years in the pages of the "Glasgow
Medical Journal," it was decided in 1895 to publish the
Transactions in volume form.  The subject had been discussed in 1893, but after making enquiries into the question of cost, the Council reported "that it would be
impossible to publish, and to continue the publication of

Transactions, worthy of the Society, under the present financial arrangements." At first it was hoped that a volume containing the joint transactions of this and of the Pathological and Clincial Society might have been arranged, but the negotiations were broken off, and the first volume of our Transactions, which contained the proceedings of sessions 1895-96 and 1896-97, appeared in due course. The succeeding volumes have been published with regularity, and duly forwarded to the members of the Society, as well as to some of the more important libraries. The publication of the Transactions of two sessions in one volume has its disadvantages, and the Council may, during the present year, submit a scheme whereby they might be published annually.

## CONGRATULATIONS TO LORD LISTER, 1897.

The following letter, addressed to Lord Lister on his elevation to the peerage, and the reply received, are of considerable interest :—

FACULTY HALL, 242 ST. VINCENT STREET,
GLASGOW, *14th February, 1897.*

To THE RIGHT HONOURABLE LORD LISTER, P.R.S.

MY LORD,—It is the desire of the Council and Members of the Glasgow Medico-Chirurgical Society to offer your Lordship their congratulations on the receipt of the honour which has been recently conferred upon you, in recognition of your distinguished scientific position, and of your valuable contributions to the sum of human welfare.

The Society recalls with much satisfaction that it had the honour to claim you as one of its members, and that its historical associations include some of the earliest records of the work which has placed your Lordship's name high on the roll of fame, and the issue of which is universally declaimed as a great and practical benediction to mankind.

In the name, and on behalf, of the Glasgow Medico-Chirurgical Society, we have the honour to subscribe ourselves,—Your Lordship's most obedient Servants,

(Signed)      W. L. REID, *President.*
(   „   )      C. O. HAWTHORNE, *Secretary.*

12 PARK CRESCENT,
LONDON, W., *18th February, 1897.*

MY DEAR DR. REID,—I beg you to convey to the Council and Members of the Medico-Chirurgical Society, my warm thanks for their most kind congratulations.—Believe me, Very sincerely yours,

(Signed)      LISTER.

### ELIGIBILITY OF LADY MEDICAL PRACTITIONERS FOR MEMBERSHIP.

At the annual general meeting of the Society held on 8th May, 1903, a recommendation from the Council, to the effect " that women who are registered medical practitioners be eligible for membership," was considered. This was put as a motion against an amendment proposing delay in the consideration of the question till the beginning of the next session. Five voted for the amendment and nine for the motion, so that " women who are registered medical practitioners be eligible for membership " was declared to be the finding of the meeting.

The first meeting of the following session was inaugurated by a heated discussion consequent on the Christian names of a lady medical practitioner having been represented on the ballot paper by initials only, and some members had voted not knowing that the candidate was otherwise than a man. As a result of the discussion the ballot papers were destroyed without counting them. This act led to further discussion, some holding that the proceedings were both irregular and unconstitutional.

Then at the first meeting in November, the following motion was submitted, viz., " That the resolution in favour of the admission of women as members of the Society, passed on 8th May, 1903, is invalid, as Rule 23 was not observed." The formalities necessary in any proposed alteration in the constitution of the Society had not been followed. When put to the vote, thirty-nine supported the motion and twenty-seven opposed it, by which vote it was declared that women were not eligible for membership of the Medico-Chirurgical Society of Glasgow.

## FUNDS.

Since the amalgamation, the subscription has remained at five shillings per annum, and there is no entrance fee. For this small subscription the member may regale himself with tea, coffee, and cakes in the Library Hall before the meeting, while he enjoys converse with his professional friends; he may attend every meeting throughout the session, keeping himself in touch with the latest developments in medicine and surgery; and at the close of every alternate session he is presented with the volume containing the transactions of the previous two sessions. Modifications have been proposed from time to time. By a payment of three guineas, life membership could at one time be assured; and in 1885 it was proposed and agreed to, that ordinary members might, if they choose, commute their annual subscription by a single payment of fifty shillings; and it was also enacted that after members had paid their annual subscription continuously for twenty years, they should be exempt from further annual contributions. This latter portion of the rule was formally deleted at the annual general meeting in May, 1891, and only those members who had by that date completed twenty continuous years of membership were entitled to the benefit.

### FAILURE OF CITY OF GLASGOW BANK, 1877.

This Society, in common with several members of our profession, suffered through the failure of the City of Glasgow Bank in 1877. Two years later it is noted in the minutes of the Council that a circular had been received from the liquidator of the City Bank, asking that the Society should forego 2s. 6d. in the pound of the money which stood at its credit in the bank when it stopped payment. The sum in the bank at that date was £96, and the Council agreed to recommend the Society to comply with the request, which was done, the abatement of the claim resulting in a loss of £11, 19s. 6d.

### PRESENT INVESTMENTS.

And at the present time, the Society, in common with investors generally, is met with a depreciation in the capital value of its reserve fund, in consequence of the lower market price of the stock in which the money is invested; but fortunately for the Society, as well as for the Corporation, whose stock we hold, the interest is paid regularly.

W. T. Gairdner

## THE GLASGOW PATHOLOGICAL AND CLINICAL SOCIETY, 1873.

This was the second Society formed in Glasgow under the designation "Pathological." The record of its formation is unusual, and no reasons are given to account for the movement. The first page of the first minute book bears the address, 152 Wellington Street, Glasgow, and the date is 25th November, 1873, and, following this, we find the heading put thus :—

*"PROPOSED*

*PATHOLOGICAL AND CLINICAL SOCIETY."*

Fifteen gentlemen were present, and "Dr. Leishman was voted to the chair ; and on his proposal a committee was appointed to prepare a draft of regulations should the formation of a Society seem desirable."

This piece of business being over, preparations, drawings, and specimens were shown by Dr. Thomas Reid, by Dr. Hector Cameron, and by Dr. John Wilson, and the meeting ended.

At the second meeting Professor Gairdner was elected president of the Society, and the other office-bearers were a vice-president and a secretary. Three years elapsed before a treasurer was appointed.

Membership was at first limited to thirty. Members were elected by ballot, and "the production of some communication by applicants must precede their election." The regular meetings were held on the second Tuesday of the month from October till May at 8 P.M., and fines for absence were imposed. "If a member is absent from three consecutive monthly meetings, a fine of five shillings shall be paid."

"Communications for the Society must be of the nature of expositions of actual facts, founded as much as possible upon objects presented for observation and criticism at the meetings.''

'' The expenses of the Society shall be defrayed by the levying of such contributions from the members as may be required.'' At first the contribution called for was five shillings; occasionally an increase was called for to defray some special outlay; and latterly the annual subscription was one of ten shillings.

The early meetings were held in the Lying-in Hospital in Wellington Street; but at the beginning of the second session, October, 1874, and on till May, 1876, this Society met in what was then spoken of as the new Eye Infirmary in Berkeley Street. From October, 1876, it met in the Faculty Hall, and continued to do so until the end.

In the second year of its existence there was trouble of a threefold character—irregular attendance, non-payment of the annual subscription, and failure to pay fines incurred. An addition was made to the laws to enable the Society to deal with such recalcitrant members. It reads thus:—'' That any member who shall have failed to attend at least four meetings of the Society during a session, or who may have failed to pay the subscription and fines incurred, shall be considered to have thereby, without further debate or vote on the subject, forfeited his membership.''

## ORDINARY MEMBERS.

When the Society was formed the number of members was, as already indicated, limited to thirty, which number was increased, however, from time to time.

In the rules published in 1879 it is intimated '' that the Society shall consist of not more than forty members.''

In 1882 the secretary intimated '' that several gentlemen were anxious to join the Society, and that there was as yet only one vacancy. After some conversation it was agreed to leave the rules as they stand, without recommending any change at present.''

In 1885 the subject of increasing the membership of the Society was again discussed, and " the Council resolved to recommend that the membership be increased by five during this session," but this proposal was negatived when discussed by the Society in March, 1885.

While the members of the Society had every right to restrict the number of members with whom they desired to be associated in the work of the Society, the position taken up by the majority resembled that of the dog in the manger, for while they themselves did not attend, they refused to admit others anxious to become members, and who if elected would have had the right to take part in the Society's proceedings.

In October, 1890, the majority relented, and it was agreed to further increase the membership. " The Society . . . shall consist of not more than fifty members."

## HONORARY MEMBERS.

In 1893 the Council desired " the power to elect honorary members up to the number of ten from the past presidents of the Society ; such elections to take place by order of seniority." The motion was agreed to by the Society in January, 1894, by four votes to two against the proposal.

## ORDINARY AND HONORARY MEMBERS.

But the arrangements did not yet give satisfaction apparently, for in May, 1897, the Council made the following proposal :—" In order to create vacancies in the Society's ordinary membership, and to render eligible as honorary members those who had not been presidents of the Society, the rule dealing with honorary members should be altered to read thus, ' that the Council has power to elect not more than three honorary members annually, such members having been connected with the Society for a period of at least twenty years.' "

### FURTHER INCREASE.

In April, 1900, it was agreed on the recommendation of the Council to increase the membership of the Society to seventy-five, and at the same meeting it was agreed that tea, coffee, etc., be provided at the meetings of the Society.

### DAYS OF MEETING—MUSIC *VERSUS* MEDICINE.

That many members of this Society preferred music to medicine might be infered from the minute of the committee meeting of date December, 1880. It is this :—
" Owing to the orchestral concerts occurring this year in December and January on the Tuesday evening, it was decided to hold the December meeting on the Wednesday following the regular night, and the January meeting either on the Monday or the Wednesday as might seem most suitable to the members when the matter was announced at next meeting."

And in 1883, " The subject of the meeting night was fully discussed again, as this last session three of the meetings having coincided with the orchestral concerts the meetings had been so far interfered with as regards attendance." It was suggested that " the meetings might be altered so as to be held on Monday nights," but it was ultimately agreed that " next session the Tuesday night be adhered to, except on the occasion of the concerts falling on the same nights, when the meetings will be held on Mondays."

The foregoing recommendation of the Council was submitted to a meeting of the Society in May, 1883, and its acceptance is minuted thus :—" The Society endorsed the recommendation of the Council as to changing the night of meeting next session to Monday when the orchestral concerts fell on the regular night of meeting, as the attendance at the meetings last session had been injuriously affected by the coincidence of these concerts."

Finally Monday was chosen as the regular day of meeting.

On 15th April, 1886, a motion by Dr. Coats was carried without any amendment, viz., " That the night of meeting of the Society be altered to the second Monday of the month in place of the second Tuesday."

## HOUR OF MEETING.

On the formation of the Society, 8 P.M. was fixed as the hour of meeting, and the Society continued to meet at that hour for close on thirty years. In October, 1897, it was proposed to change the hour of meeting to 4.30 P.M., but the proposal was not then entertained. In October, 1902, however, the Council discussed means whereby the attendance might be increased. One was that there should be a greater number and variety of items on each billet, and the other was a change in the hour of meeting.

The president called attention to the very small proportion of members constituting an ordinary attendance at meetings of the Society, and advocated an alteration of the hour of meeting with a view to improve this. He suggested that the hour be changed to 4.30 P.M. as an experiment, and proposed that this be stated on the billet for the first meeting, as a recommendation from the Council, which was agreed to.

The recommendation was placed before the Society on 10th November, 1902. After discussion it was agreed to adopt 4.30 P.M. as the hour of meeting for the remainder of that session.

On 10th April, 1903, it was agreed by Council to recommend that 4.30 be the hour of meeting for the next session, although one member advocated alternate meetings at 4.30 and 8.30, which proposal was not entertained by the Council. At the meeting of the Society in May, the proposal of the Council was agreed to, though an amendment to return to the former hour of meeting (8 P.M.) was proposed and defeated.

F

On 11th April, 1904, it was moved that the hour of
meeting of the Society for the future be 4.30 P.M.    But
an amendment to the effect that the former hour of
meeting, viz., 8 o'clock, be adhered to, was proposed;
and when the vote was taken, it was declared that only
three had voted for the motion, and eleven for the amendment in favour of the evening hour.

At the beginning of the next session (October, 1904),
it was proposed that the regular meetings of the Society
should be held on the evening of the second Monday of
the month, at 8.30 P.M., which proposal was unanimously
agreed to at the next ordinary meeting.    And 8.30 P.M.
remained the hour of meeting until the Society became
merged in the Medico-Chirurgical Society.


## FUNDS.

In 1884 it is noted in making up the budget for the year
that a sum of £5, 15s. was derived from fines exacted
from members for non-attendance; and at the same
time, to clear the cost of a volume of Transactions
about to be published, it was resolved that the subscription for the year be raised to 15s.

In the following year the subscription was fixed at 10s.

In the treasurer's report for 1885-86 the receipts
amounted to £24, 17s. 11d., while the expenditure
amounted to £48, 18s. 7d., leaving a debt of £24, 0s. 8d.
due by the Society, and the Council resolved to recommend
that the subscription be fixed at one pound for next session.

The increase in the expenditure was due to the publication of the Transactions of the Society, to having a paid
reporter at the meetings, and to the reprinting and circu-
lating the discussion on albuminuria in 1884, and on cancer
in 1886.

A committee was appointed to enquire into the question
generally, and amongst other things it recommended an
increase in the membership, that fines for non-attendance

be abolished, that the annual subscription be fixed at ten shillings, and the publication of Transactions be placed under the charge of a special committee.

The increase in the numbers of the membership was not agreed to by the Society, and in May, 1887, it was resolved, on the motion of Dr. Robertson, that the publication of Transactions in a separate volume should be discontinued for the present.

Further evidence of the waning interest of the members in the work of the Society is indicated in the following abstract from the minutes of 2nd October, 1902 :—" The treasurer stated that as a result of a circular issued early in September he had received £11, 10s. as arrears of subscriptions due. There were, however, thirty-five members whose subscriptions were in arrears for periods varying from one to four sessions."

## DECLINES THE PRESIDENCY.

Professor Macewen, who was an original member of this Society, was nominated by the Council for the presidency in 1885. But just prior to the day of election, although his was the only name proposed, he intimated his desire not to accept the office.

## SIR WILLIAM T. GAIRDNER.

Sir William attended the Society for the last time at the opening meeting of session 1902-1903, when he expressed the pleasure it gave him to be present. He had always cherished an active interest in the Society, he said, and continued to do so, for as the first president he had been associated with all the senior members of the Society. He emphasised the function of the Society as being essentially a working one.

## PUBLICATION OF THE TRANSACTIONS.

Complete reports of the Transactions of the Society appeared regularly in the pages of the " Glasgow Medical Journal " during the first eleven years. In addition, abstracts were published from time to time in the " Lancet " and the " British Medical Journal."

In 1883 the Council resolved that the reports then appearing in the " Glasgow Medical Journal " should be collected and published as a separate volume of Transactions. The first volume, containing a full record of the business transacted by the Society during session 1883-1884, was published in September, 1884; the second volume, containing the transactions for two sessions, appeared in 1886, and then their publication ceased.

In 1891 it was again decided to publish a volume of Transactions, embracing the work of the five years from 1886 to 1891 ; but the material being too much to be published in one volume, it was further decided by the Society that only a portion of its Transactions during those five years should be included, and a committee of selection was appointed.

The publication of the fifth volume (1893-95) was delayed by the death of the editor, Dr. John Carslaw. In the preface it is stated that " the Transactions are a posthumous record of the painstaking and thoroughness with which they were compiled and edited, and that the Society loses in Dr. Carslaw, not only a valued member, but an editor and reporter of its Transactions whose place it will be difficult adequately to fill."

From that date onwards the Transactions have appeared regularly, each volume containing a record of the work of the two preceding sessions; and the eleventh volume, which is now in the press, will close the record of the work of the Glasgow Pathological and Clinical Society as a separate Society.

### ADMISSION OF LADY MEDICALS TO MEMBERSHIP.

While some lady medicals were knocking at the door of the Medico-Chirurgical Society, others were longing to become members of the Pathological and Clinical. The first formal note of the fact occurring in the minutes was the intimation of the following notice of motion, which was read from the chair at the meeting held on 12th October, 1903 :—'' That ladies possessed of the necessary medical qualifications may be admitted to the membership of this Society.''

This motion was discussed at the following meeting, held on 9th November. The gentleman in whose name the motion stood said '' that a lady practitioner was engaged in his wards in the study of the pathology of the pelvic organs. As it was his desire that she might be in a position to present her work before this Society, he was obliged to bring up this motion.'' In the subsequent discussion some expressed the opinion that the character of the meetings would be altered by the admission of ladies, and that its usefulness would be limited. '' It must be borne in mind,'' one said, '' that the Society is a clinical as well as a pathological one, and that at times the cases of patients are presented to the Society whose complete demonstration would, in the presence of lady members, constitute a real difficulty.'' Others, who had given clinical instruction to mixed classes, had experienced none of the objections raised ; and another '' could not perceive any difference between the presence of a nurse and a lady practitioner, during the demonstrations of particular cases.''

When the motion for the admission of lady practitioners to the membership of the Society was put to the meeting, twelve voted for and seven voted against it, and the motion was thereupon declared carried. This finding was immediately followed by notice of motion, '' That the rules of the Society requiring alteration, be modified to

include lady members.'' This motion was discussed at
the next meeting, and there being no amendment, the
necessary changes in the wording of the rules were
arranged.

While this change in the constitution of the Society was
carried, no change in the character of its membership
resulted. There is no note in the minutes of any lady
having been proposed for membership, and certainly none
were ever admitted to membership. But it is recorded
that on the 12th November, 1906, a lady practitioner,
introduced by a member, gave '' a lantern demonstration
on primary carcimoma of the ovary.''

## AMALGAMATION WITH THE MEDICO-CHIRURGICAL SOCIETY, 1907.

The Pathological and Clinical Society was primarily a
Society of workers, and each member was expected to con-
tribute of his best each year. And during the thirty-three
years which was the measure of its life, it has been an
important factor in the diffusion of knowledge of facts,
newly discovered and known of old, bearing on the science
and practice of medicine and surgery.

In recent years it has been felt that there was considerable overlapping in the work done by the Pathological
and the Medico-Chirurgical Societies, and as the
attendance of members at the former had seriously fallen
off, members were tempted to take their specimens and
communications to a society where they would be seen by
a larger number. As a consequence the number and,
perhaps, the importance of the contributions had also
suffered of late. For these reasons it was felt by the
Council of the Pathological and Clinical Society that it
would be advantageous to join forces with the Medico-
Chirurgical Society, and accordingly on 20th September,
1906, '' it was remitted to the president and the secretary
to sound the Medico-Chirurgical Society on the question,

and, if their reply was favourable, to carry out the necessary arrangements for bringing the matter before an
ordinary meeting of this Society at an early date."

The subject was brought before the Council of the
Medico-Chirurgical Society, and an informal discussion
took place at a meeting of Council on 5th October, 1906,
at which "it was resolved to agree generally with the
object of the proposal, but without committing the Council
or the Society in any way as to terms."

The subject was very fully discussed at several subsequent meetings of the Pathological and Clinical Society,
and amalgamation was finally agreed to, practically unanimously.  Then, in February, 1907, a deputation from the
Pathological and Clinical Society was received, and its
representations considered, respecting a proposal made
by that Society for amalgamation with the Medico-
Chirurgical.  During the discussion it was mentioned that
only two or three members of the Pathological were not at
the same time members of the Medico-Chirurgical Society,
so that the actual question of amalgamation became
narrowed down to the absorption by the Medico-
Chirurgical Society into its membership of those gentlemen, and the perpetuation in some way of the name of the
Pathological and Clinical Society.

Our Council reported the result of the conferences which
had taken place between it and the committee appointed
by the Pathological and Clinical Society relative to the
proposed amalgamation to this Society at its meeting held
on 1st March, 1907.  The result is thus recorded :—" This
Society cordially approves of the proposal made to it by
the Pathological and Clinical Society for amalgamation of
the two societies," and at the same meeting the Council
was authorised " to confer with the Council of the Pathological Society and to formulate terms of amalgamation in
time for these being finally approved at the next statutory
meeting in April."  The agreement arrived at was communicated to the Society under three heads—the first

dealt with the date, " that amalgamation shall take effect from the beginning of next winter session " ; the second arranged for the appointment of a committee for the purchase of apparatus for pathological demonstrations ; and the third related to a commemorative note.

To perpetuate the memory of the Pathological and Clinical Society, it was arranged that the words, " Glasgow Pathological and Clinical Society amalgamated 1907," be printed on the billets and official paper of the Medico-Chirurgical Society, immediately below the present heading, and, further, that in the next issue of the rules opportunity should be taken to insert a suitable historical notice of the Pathological and Clinical Society and the work it accomplished.

There were but four members of the Pathological Society who were not also members of the Medico-Chirurgical Society, so the amalgamation did not appreciably add to our numbers, for at the close of last session we had 416 members on our roll. Neither have our funds been augmented, for it was agreed that, whatever surplus remained in the hands of the treasurer of the Pathological Society when all accounts had been paid, should be spent in the purchase of apparatus for the use of this Society.

## PRESIDENTS.

Any detailed history of the many men who have presided over the deliberations of this Society since 1814 would be impossible in the time at my disposal, and as some account of most of them is given by Dr Duncan, repetition by me would serve no useful purpose.     But I will refer very briefly to the first president of each of the various Societies which by their amalgamation have led to the formation of the large and flourishing Society which it is my privilege to address to-night.

### THE GLASGOW MEDICAL SOCIETY, 1814.

Robert Watt, M.D., the first president of the Glasgow Medical Society, was born in the parish of Stewarton in 1774, and in the intervals of labour on the farm and as a stonemason he qualified himself to begin his University course.   After having practised for a short time in Paisley, he settled in Glasgow in a house in Queen Street as a physician, and became a successful lecturer on the theory and practice of medicine, forming a library for the use of his students.   He died at the age of 45, and yet in that short life he rose to the presidency of the Faculty of Physicians and Surgeons, became a physician to the Royal Infirmary, and published several important works entailing extensive research.   His " Bibliotheca Britannica," which is described by Dr. Duncan as " one of the most stupendous monuments existing of the patient labour of a single man," was completed before his death, though he died before its publication.

### THE MEDICO-CHIRURGICAL SOCIETY OF GLASGOW, 1844.

Thomas Thomson, M.D., Fellow of the Royal Society and Regius Professor of Chemistry in the University of Glasgow, was born in Crieff in 1774.   He was elected to the presidency of the Medical Society in 1826, in succession to Dr. Robert Perry, and he held that office till 1829. He was elected first president of the Medico-Chirurgical Society in 1844, and remained in office for two years.  He was editor of the third edition of the " Encyclopædia Britannica " ;  was appointed Regius Professor of Chemistry in the University of Glasgow in 1818; and for two years he was one of the physicians to the Royal Infirmary.   Amongst several works, he published a " System of Chemistry," which passed through several editions.   In his teaching he introduced a system of symbols, and he was the inventor of the oxy-hydrogen blow-pipe.

At the ceremony connected with the opening of the new laboratories at our University in April of the present year, the attention of the Prince of Wales was directed to the fact " that the first chemical laboratory for students was established in 1830 at the University of Glasgow by Professor Thomas Thomson, several years before the foundation of Liebig's celebrated laboratory at Giesen."   He died in 1852.

### FIRST PRESIDENT AFTER AMALGAMATION, 1866.

Dr. Allen Thomson was the first president of the Society after the amlgamation of 1866.  He was the son of Prof. John Thomson, of Edinburgh, where he was born in 1809.  Throughout his professional life he was associated with the teaching of anatomy.  Working at first with Mr. William Sharpey in Edinburgh, he was successively elected to the professorship of Anatomy in Aberdeen, the professorship of Institutes of Medicine in Edinburgh University, and lastly to the professorship of Anatomy in the University of Glasgow.  Many of us still remember him as the kindly and courteous gentleman who was the first University professor to address us when on the threshold of our medical career.  He did much to establish our University on Gilmorehill, and he ever had the deepest interest in all that pertained to its welfare. Besides being a Doctor of Medicine, he was a Fellow, a member of the Council, and a vice-president of the Royal Society; he was an honorary Fellow of the Faculty of Physicians and Surgeons of Glasgow; and the honorary degree of LL.D. was conferred upon him by the Universities of both Glasgow and Edinburgh. Further, he was president of the British Association in 1877. He died in 1884.

## THE GLASGOW PATHOLOGICAL AND CLINICAL SOCIETY, 1873.

Sir William T. Gairdner, who was the first president of the Pathological and Clinical Society, was born in Edinburgh in 1824, and since last we met as a Society in this hall he has passed away. To many of us he was the ideal physician, and his presence was heartily welcomed at meetings of our Society, whether as president (he was president of the Medico-Chirurgical Society from 1882-1884) or simply as a member, for no man could so readily illume any subject under discussion, and his remarks were ever eloquent and instructive. Many honours were conferred upon him: he was a Fellow of the Royal Society, a Doctor of Laws, a Knight Commander of the Bath, and each and all were so fully deserved that their bestowal gave pleasure to every member of his profession who knew him. As a teacher he was unrivalled; as a speaker he was ever interesting; as a man he was without guile, the soul of honour, and of well-reasoned religious convictions. His learning was so extensive and profound that it has been said of him he was fitted to occupy any chair in the University; and as a physician it is recorded that a recognised authority once remarked, "I regard Gairdner as the first physician in Europe." Although laid aside from active work for some years, his was the outstanding name and figure in the medical life of our city for a full generation— and we may never look upon his like again.

## LIST OF PRESIDENTS.

I. THE GLASGOW MEDICAL SOCIETY,
1814.

| Session. | President. |
|---|---|
| 1814–15 | Robert Watt. |
| 1815–16 | James Monteath. |
| 1816–17 | William Couper. |
| 1817–18 | T. Brown. |
| 1818–19 | Robert Graham. |
| 1819–20 | George Macleod. |
| 1820–21 | James Watson. |
| 1821–22 | G. C. Monteath. |
| 1822–23 | John Baird. |
| 1823–24 | Thomas Thomson. |
| 1824–25 | William Cumin. |
| 1825–26 | Robert Perry. |
| 1826–27 | Thomas Thomson. |
| 1827–28 | Thomas Thomson. |
| 1828–29 | Thomas Thomson. |
| 1829–30 | Thomas Thomson. |
| 1830–31 | William Young. |
| 1831–32 | William Young. |
| 1832–33 | James Wilson. |
| 1833–34 | James Wilson. |
| 1834–35 | John Macfarlane. |
| 1835–36 | John Macfarlane. |
| 1836–37 | John Macfarlane. |
| 1837–38 | Andrew Buchanan. |
| 1838–39 | Andrew Buchanan. |
| 1839–40 | Robert Cowan. |
| 1840–41 | William Weir. |
| 1841–42 | William Weir. |
| 1842–43 | A. J. Hannay. |
| 1843–44 | A. J. Hannay. |
| 1844–45 | Robert Perry. |
| 1845–46 | J. Wilson. |
| 1846–47 | William Lyon. |
| 1847–48 | George Watson. |
| 1848–49 | George Watson. |
| 1849–50 | J. A. Easton. |
| 1850–51 | R. G. Maxwell. |
| 1851–52 | James Wilson. |
| 1852–53 | James Wilson. |
| 1853–54 | James Wilson. |
| 1854–55 | James Wilson. |

II. THE MEDICO-CHIRURGICAL SOCIETY
OF GLASGOW, 1844.

| Session. | President. |
|---|---|
| 1844–46 | Thomas Thomson. |
| 1846–48 | Harry Rainy. |
| 1848–50 | A. D. Anderson. |
| 1850–52 | James Watson. |
| 1852–54 | Andrew Buchanan. |
| 1854–56 | James Wilson. |

## LIST OF PRESIDENTS (*continued*).

**I. The Glasgow Medical Society,**
1814 (*continued*).

| Session. | President. |
|---|---|
| 1855–56 | William Lyon. |
| 1856–57 | Joseph Bell. |
| 1857–58 | J. G. Fleming. |
| 1858–59 | George Watt. |
| 1859–60 | William Brown. |
| 1860–61 | James Fraser. |
| 1861–62 | John Reid. |
| 1862–63 | James Adams. |
| 1863–64 | James Stewart. |
| 1864–65 | James Morton. |
| 1865–66 | G. H. B. Macleod. |

**II. The Medico–Chirurgical Society**
of Glasgow, 1844 (*continued*).

| Session. | President. |
|---|---|
| 1856–58 | James A. Lawrie. |
| 1858–60 | William Weir. |
| 1860–62 | John M. Pagan. |
| 1862–64 | William Lyon. |
| 1864–66 | Charles Ritchie. |

**III. Societies amalgamated (1866)**
under name of
The Medico–Chirurgical Society
of Glasgow.

| Session. | President. |
|---|---|
| 1866–68 | Allen Thomson. |
| 1868–70 | J. G. Fleming. |
| 1870–72 | James Adams. |
| 1872–74 | Robert Scott Orr. |
| 1874–76 | James Morton. |
| 1876–78 | Ebenezer Watson. |
| 1878–80 | Andrew Fergus. |
| 1880–82 | George Buchanan. |
| 1882–84 | W. T. Gairdner. |
| 1884–87 | G. H. B. Macleod. |
| 1887–89 | T. M'Call Anderson. |
| 1889–91 | William Macewen. |
| 1891–93 | Joseph Coats. |
| 1893–95 | Hector C. Cameron. |
| 1895–97 | William L. Reid. |
| 1897–99 | George S. Middleton. |
| 1899–1901 | Henry E. Clark. |
| 1901–1903 | W. G. Dun. |
| 1903–1905 | David Newman. |
| 1905–1907 | J. Lindsay Steven. |

**IV. The Glasgow Pathological and**
Clinical Society, 1873.

| Session. | President. |
|---|---|
| 1873–76 | W. T. Gairdner. |
| 1876–78 | Joseph Coats. |
| 1878–80 | Alexander Robertson. |
| 1880–82 | Hector C. Cameron. |
| 1882–84 | T. M'Call Anderson. |
| 1884–86 | George Buchanan. |
| 1886–88 | James Finlayson. |
| 1888–90 | W. T. Gairdner. |
| 1890–92 | David Newman. |
| 1892–94 | Samson Gemmell. |
| 1894–96 | D. N. Knox. |
| 1896–98 | Donald Fraser. |
| 1898–99 | William James Fleming. |
| 1899–1900 | Thomas Barr. |
| 1900–1902 | Henry E. Clark. |
| 1902–1904 | A. E. Maylard. |
| 1904–1906 | Robert Muir. |
| 1906–1907 | J. Lindsay Steven. |

**V. Societies United, 1907.**

## THANKS TO THE SOCIETY.

And now, having spoken of the long and honourable career pursued by this Society, and having made mention of but a few of the many eminent men who have presided over its deliberations, I wish to thank you, the present-day members of this Society, representatives of a long line of honourable professional men, for the great honour you have conferred upon me in electing me to be your president.  I assure you that I appreciate the honour very highly.  But the feeling of happiness, consequent on my election to the chair, is turned to a spirit of heaviness when I think of and compare myself with the many outstanding members of our profession who have occupied the same post in days gone by, and who each felt honoured in being called to the presidency.  Further, I take up the reins of office with much trepidation, following immediately, as I do, Dr. John Lindsay Steven, who was one of the most popular presidents of recent times, a man well versed in the conduct of public meetings, full of knowledge relating to medical education, a keen debater, and an eloquent speaker.  As I am lacking in these qualifications, I desire in taking office to bespeak your forbearance, and to ask your hearty support in the work of the Society during my term of office.  This Society, while it has on its roll of membership almost every physician and surgeon who is a teacher in the world-famous school of medicine of Glasgow, is largely composed of men engaged in general practice.  I, on the other hand, am one of a smaller band, the members of which have chosen to practise in a special department of surgery, and so as a specialist, and thus one of a numericaly small, though not now a despised, set, I accept my election as a compliment, and as a source of encouragement, to those who, like myself, have embraced specialism.

## CLOSING REMARKS.

This Society has great traditions, and a history of which we may well be proud. Like other institutions similarly constituted, it has had its periods of prosperity and its times of adversity. It has been privileged to number amongst its ordinary members—members who took a prominent part in its proceedings—the greatest man in modern surgery, besides many others whose names are now inseparably associated with the advance of medicine and the successful entrance of surgery into regions which were in former times looked upon as inaccessible to his knife or trephine.

At times this Society has lent its moral support— yes, and sometimes its pecuniary help—to aid some project beneficial to the profession or to check some proposed action by those in authority which seemed likely to wrongfully damage the status of the profession or of an individual member of it. Yet these excursions into what might be termed the political arena were few; and though tempted in later years to take part in medical political movements it has sternly refused; and if we desire to uphold the traditions handed down to us and to make progress on scientific lines, we must keep our Society absolutely free from medical politics and from everything savouring of trades-unionism. In the study of the science of medicine and surgery and its application to practice, we have a sufficiently large field to occupy all our energies and all the time at our disposal.

Whether we should be content to pursue our work under the same designation as heretofore, or seek to bring about an amalgamation of other Societies in Glasgow doing similar work, and found an Academy of Medicine and Surgery, or make application for a Royal Charter, as was suggested by Dr. Ritchie in 1865, is for the Society to determine.

Meantime, I would urge the more regular attendance of the members at our ordinary meetings, for be he physician, surgeon, general practitioner, or specialist, he will learn, if he intelligently follows the routine proceedings of the Society, that others besides himself are striving to do good, useful, and noble work: and possibly he may in turn, from the abundance of his knowledge, help to instruct others.

" Experience keeps a dear school," but the experience which teaches must not of necessity be our own personal experience; it may be purchased at the expense of our neighbours; and at our meetings we learn of, and by, the experience of others in all departments of medicine and surgery, which tuition, if we be apt pupils, will be to our advantage, and to the advantage of those placed under our care.